211 .

56
Supt.

Antoinette, Baroness De Poly

SEMPER FIDELIS

REGI

Mrs Stevens Bradfu

MEMOIRS

OF THE

FAMILY DE POLY,

WITH A

NARRATIVE OF THE LIFE

OF

ANTOINETTE BARONESS DE POLY,

WRITTEN BY HERSELF.

Loyal au Mort.

𝔑orthampton:

PRINTED AND PUBLISHED BY J. ABEL.

1822.

TO

THE GENEROUS, HUMANE, AND MOST BENEVOLENT

PUBLIC,

FROM WHOM THE ORPHAN HAS, IN A FOREIGN LAND,

RECEIVED   INNUMERABLE   BENEFITS,

THIS WORK

IS,

MOST   HUMBLY,   MOST   RESPECTFULLY,

AND

MOST   GRATEFULLY

Dedicated,

BY

THE AUTHOR.

571

PREFACE.

THE first fifty pages of this work having been originally composed during the French Revolution,—a period, in which, inviolable secrecy with respect to names and places was indispensably necessary; the names in the Manuscript were allowed to be expressed only by their initial letters : it has since, however, been deemed desirable, in order to give weight to the truth of these Memoirs, that this defect should be in some way supplied, and therefore the Editor, by permission of the Baroness, begs leave to insert those of her father in full length, as under :—

At page 2, 8th line from the note, instead of " The Baron de K....., son of Louis Baron de K.....," read " Frederick Charles Guillaume Leonard Bàron de Poly de Kallenback, son of Louis Baron de Kallenback."

But not being able satisfactorily to fill up the rest, it has been thought preferable, rather than commit any error, to retain them precisely as in the Manuscript.

The translation also, of this part of the Memoirs, from the French, is as strictly literal as the languages will admit ; but since translation should be the act of rendering ideas, and not merely words, from one language into another, such liberties have been occasionally taken as were considered necessary to keep up the spirit of the original, without deviating from the sense of the author. How far the translator has succeeded in these respects, it is not her province to decide ; conscious that egotism is too partial to deserve approbation, she cheerfully submits her labours to the opinion of an impartial, liberal, and discerning public, having for so many years past experienced their liberality and munificence.

BANBURY,
NOVEMBER 1st, 1822.

Names of the Subscribers.

————⟫⟫⟩●⟨⟪⟪————

A.

LADY Arundle, Wardour-Castle, 2 copies
Mrs. B. Aplin, Bodicott mansion
Benjamin Aplin, Esq. London
Weston Aplin, Esq. Chipping Norton
Miss Armetriding, Steeple-Ashton
Mrs. Attenbrow, Stratton-Audley
Mr. George Ashness, London
Mrs. Austin, Banbury
Mrs. Arnold, Brackley
Mr. Adams, Fritwell
Mr. W. Arne, Banbury
Miss Aston, Rowington Hall

B.

The Rev. Edward Burn, Birmingham
Monsieur L'Abbe Bertomier, London, 2 copies
The Rev. Henry Leigh Bennett, Croughton
Mrs. Blencowe, Marston, 2 copies
Miss Basset, Tehidy Park, Cornwall
Miss M. Basset, Ditto
Mrs. James Blencowe, Pengreep, Cornwall
Mrs. Bowen, Wroxton Abbey
Mrs. Burgess, Straton-Audley
Miss Bentom, London
Miss Botrey, Marston
Miss Biddle, Prescott

Mrs. Richard Bignell, Middleton-Stoney
Mrs. Bawcutt
Miss Brett, Sloane Street, London
Mrs. Bull, Hanwell
Miss Bull, Ditto
Robert Brayne, Esq. Banbury
Mrs. Beasant, Old Stratford
Mr. Horatio Bolingbroke, Norwich
Mr. Bristow, Bodicott
Philip Bartlett, Esq. Buckingham
J. Bartlett, Esq. Ditto
T. Bartlett, Esq. Ditto
Mrs. Brickwell, Banbury
Mr. Bristow, Kidlington.
Mr. Baker, Market-Deeping
E. Bartlett, Esq. Buckingham
Miss Bartlett, Ditto
Mrs. E. Bartlett, Brackley
Mrs. R. Bartlett, Ditto
Mrs. Bartlett, Deddington
Mrs. Barford, Banbury
Mrs. Busby, Ditto
Mr. Thomas Batchelor, Middleton-Cheney
Mr. Samuel Beesley, Banbury
Mr. Barrett, Brackley
Mrs. Bannard, Fulwell
The Rev. Mr. Bell, Bloxham
The Rev. W. E. Bottomley, Middleton-Cheney
Miss Bellamy, Shipston
Mrs. Brain, Ditto
Mr. John Burchley, Cropredy
Mrs. Bowles, North-Aston
Mrs. Bygrave, Deddington
Mrs. Edward Bates, Bloxham
Mrs. Bartholomew, Wardington
Mr. William Budd, Boddington
The Rev. A. Browley, Leamington
Mrs. Bird, Ditto
Miss Biddle, Prescott
Mr. C. Beavan, Master of the Leamington Ceremonies
Mrs. Burman, Southam
Edward Bouverie. Esq. Delapre Abbey
Mrs. Bouverie, Ditto
Mrs. Burnham, Northampton
Messrs. Birdsall and Sons, Northampton

Mrs. Bullock, Cayessfield, 2 copies
Mr. W. Ball, Bicester
Dr. Bourne, Oxford
The Rev. Dr. Barnes, Ditto

C.

Earl Compton
Countess Compton
Lady Elizabeth Compton
Miss Cleplane
Madame la Comtesse de Callone, London
Thomas Carter, Esq. Edgcott
Bryan Cooke, Esq. Owston, near Doncaster
The Rev. Charles Cornelius Chambers, Rector of
    Holmpton, &c. &c. &c. Holderness
The Rev. Mr. Churton, Middleton
Mrs. Chandler, Willaston
William Cooper, Esq. Ramsgate, 2 copies
Mrs. Timothy Cobb, Banbury, 2 copies
Miss Cobb, Colthrope-House
William Coles, Esq. Bicester
Mrs. Churchill, Ditto
Mrs. Clarson, Adderbury
Miss Clarke, Barton
Mrs. Carpenter, Bourne-Heath, Worcestershire
Miss Claridge, London
Miss Coates, Wappingham
Mrs. Corney, London, 2 copies
Mr. Colebrook
Miss Colebrook
Miss Hariet Colebrook
Mr. Campion, Moor-Hill
Mrs. Coles, Stratton-Audley
Mrs. Clements, Bicester
Mr. Crakenthorpe, London
Mrs. H. Churchill, Deddington.
W. H. Chamberlain, Esq. Cropredy-Lawn, 2 copies
Miss Churchill, Deddington, 2 copies
Mrs. John Churchill, Deddington
Mrs. R. Colisson, Brackley
Mrs. Cave, Ditto
Miss Cave, Ditto
Mr. James Collingridge, Fritwell

Miss Copps, Royal Hotel, Leamington
Mr. Croome, Banbury
Miss Cork, Ditto
Mr. George Craddock, Sulgrave
Mrs. Colbourne, Shipston
George Cobb, Esq. Broughton Castle
Mr. Amos Chinner, Sen. Chacombe
Miss Clements, No. 7, Hill-street, Berkeley-square
Miss Coles, Southam
Samuel Chase, Esq. Northampton
Rev. Dr. Coplestone, Oriel-College, Oxford
Rev. Dr. Collinson, Oxford
Mrs. Collingwood, Oxford
Mrs. Coles, Woodstock

D

The Right Hon. Lord de Dunstanville, Tehidy Park, Cornwall, 2 copies
Lady de Dunstanville, Ditto Ditto
Sir English Dolben, Bart. Finedon-Manor, Northamptonshire
Cotterell Dormer, Esq. Rousham
Mrs. Davis, Adderbury
Mr. C. W. Drury, Banbury
The Rev. Henry Davis, Bloxham
Mrs. William Davis, Ditto
Mrs. Davis, Banbury
Mrs. Dudley, Chapel-House
Mrs. Darville, Banbury
Mrs. Drake, Finsbury-place, London
Miss Dudley, Oxford
Mrs. Depuis, Oxford, 2 copies
Mrs. Davenport, St. Giles's, Oxford
—— Davis, Esq. Bicester, 2 copies

E.

The Countess of Erine, at the Right Hon. the Earl of Liverpool's Fife House
Mrs. Eyre, London
Mrs. Eliss, Middleton-Cheney
Mr. Edwards, Banbury

W. G. Elliston. Esq. Leamington
John Earthorpe, Esq. Cadogan-place
Rev. B. L. Edwards, Northampton
Mr. William Eagles, Cropredy

F.

Lady Gertrude Fitzpatrick, Farning-woods
Lady Ann Fitzpatrick
A Friend, Adderbury
The Rev. Thomas Fawcett, Aynho
Mrs. Ford, Bath
Mr. Freeman, Hardwick
Miss Frier, London
Miss Farndon, Deddington
Mrs. Fences, Aylesbury-House, Warwickshire
Mrs. Florers, Whitchurch
Mr. Franklin, Leamington
A Friend, in Banbury
The Rev. Dr. Fatham, Lincoln College, Oxford
J. Fane, Esq. M. P. Oxford

G.

The Right Hon. the Earl of Guilford, Wroxton
   Abbey, 4 copies
Countess of Guilford, Ditto, 2 copies
Lord Glenbervie, 2 copies
Mrs. Gother, London
Miss Gother, Ditto
Mrs. Gander, Ditto
Miss Golby, Banbury, 2 copies
Miss Greaves, Abthorpe
Mrs. Gunn, Neithorpe
Mrs. Greaves, Manor-House, Haversham
Mrs. Gee, Brackley
Mrs. Gillet, Brailes
Mrs. Gardner, Adderbury
Miss Gardner, Balscott
Mrs. Green, Brackley
Mr. J. Goode, Buckingham
Mr. Richard Garrett, Eydon
Miss S. M. Gulliver, Banbury

Mrs. Goode, Buckingham
A Gentleman, Adderbury, 2 copies
Mr. John Garrett, Calcott-Cottage, Heyford
Mrs. Griffin, Banbury
Mrs. G. Grimbly, Ditto.
Mr. John Gulliver, Ditto
Miss Susan Guttridge, Thorpe-Mandeville
Mr. James Garrett, Banbury
Miss Golley, Ditto
James Wake Golby, Esq. Ditto
Miss Goodman, Willscott
Mr. S. A. Gillet, Shipston
The Rev. William Gorden, Dunstew
Miss Griffin, Deddington
Miss Goddard, Brondstone
Miss Ann Gunn, Neithorpe
Mrs. Graves, Ditto
The Rev. R. J. Geldart, Rector of Little-Billing
Mrs. Goodacre, Northampton
W. Gates, Esq. Ditto

H

Thomas Hunt, Esq. Stratford-on-Avon
William Hunter, Esq. Leamington
Mrs. F. Hutton, Northiam, Sussex
Miss Hatton, Walkworth
Mrs. Hillyard, Thorplands-House, near Northampton
The Rev. John Hill, High-street, Oxford
Mrs. Hanks, Oxford
Sir Edward Hitchings, Oxford
The Rev. J. W. Hughes, Oxford
Mrs. Hastings, Dalesford-House, 3 copies
Mrs. Hopcraft, Croughton-House, 3 copies
Mrs. Heydon, Banbury, 2 copies
Miss Hopcraft, Evenley
Miss S. Hopcroft, Ditto
Miss Horwood, Steane-Park
Miss Holloway, Manor-House, Buckingham
Mrs. Hughes, Shennington
Mrs. Hetherington, Whitchurch
Mrs. Hollingridge, Heath
Mr. W. Hitchcock, Banbury, 2 copies
Miss Hitchcock, Ditto

Mrs. Hemmingway, Chichester
Miss Hirons, Sidnum
Miss Heath, Newington, London
Mrs. H......, London
Mrs. Humphrey, Thorpe-Mandeville
Thomas Hearne, Jun. Esq. Buckingham
The Rev. W. Harding, Sulgrave
The Rev. Mr. Hubbard, Banbury
Mrs. Hawtyn, Ditto
——— Hickman, Esq. Market-Deeping
Mr. William Hitchman, Chipping-Norton
Mrs. Hoare, Brackley
Mr. John Heath, Chipping-Norton
Mrs. Hayward, Ditto
Mr. Samuel Hickvale, Over-Norton
Mr. W. Haynes, Adderbury
Mr. John Hawkes, Sulgrave
Mr. William Hill, North-Aston
Mrs. J. Holloway, Wickham
Mrs. Richard Holloway, Bloxham
Richard Hirons, Esq. Chacombe
Mrs. Hall, Shipston
The Rev. P. Hersent, Overthorpe
Miss Harris, Deddington
The Rev. Nicks Marshall Hacker, Enstone
The Rev. W. E. Honey, South-Newington
Mrs. Harrison, Banbury
Mrs. Robert Hemming, Ditto

I.

Major General Sir Charles Inchiff, London
Lady Inchiff, Ditto
Mrs. Ingram, Thenford-House, 4 copies
Mrs. B. Ingram, Ditto, 2 copies
Miss Irons, Stratton-Audley
Miss Ivies, London
Mrs. Isted, Ecton
The Countess of Jersey, Middleton-Park
Mrs. Johnson, Thenford-House
Adolphus Johnson, Esq. London, 2 copies
The Rev. Anselm Jones, Brackley
Miss Johstiney, Buckingham
Mr. R. R. Judd, Birmingham
Mr. Jeanings, Somerton

Charles Jones, Esq. Surgeon, Banbury
Mrs. Jones, Brackley
Mr. Jones, Overthorpe
William Jeffs, Esq. Costow-House
Miss Jelf, Castle-Ashby
Mrs. E. Jones, Southam
The Rev. Humphrey Jeston, Rector of Avon-Dessel
Mr. James, Albion-Hall, Oxford

K.

Sir Charles Knightley, Bart. Fawsley-Park
Mrs. Kekewich, Newington
Mrs. Kimingway
Mrs. Kirby, Bicester
Mr. Thomas Kilby, Banbury
Master W. G. King, Avon-Dasset
Mr. G. Kalabargo, Banbury
Mrs. Burrows Kirby, Ditto

L.

Sir Henry Lawson, Brough-Hall, near Catterick, 2 copies
Lady Lawson, Ditto, 2 copies
Sir George Leigh, Hartwell-House, 6 copies
The Rev. Mr. Lancaster, Vicar of Banbury
Mrs. M. Longe, Banbury, 2 copies
Mrs. Lloyd, Middleton-Cheney
John Lewis, Esq. Old-Post, near Oswestry
Mrs. R. W. Leonard, Aynho
Mrs. H. Lucas, Newport-Pagnell
Mr. Richard Lovell, Edgcott
Mrs. Lamb, Shelswell
—— Lever, Esq. Surgeon, Culworth
Master Lewis, Droughton-House
Mr. William Loftus, Banbury
Mrs. Anthony Longe, Banbury, 2 copies
James Little, Esq. R. N. Stonehouse, Plymouth, Devon.
Mr. Joseph Langford, Burghfield-Reading
Mrs. Loveday, Wilscot
A Lady, London
A Lady, Charwelton, Northamptonshire
Monsieur de Lalande, Northampton
Lady Lock, Oxford
Mr. Laurent, St. Clements, Oxford

Mrs. Landon, Worster-College, Oxford
Mr. William Lucas, Bicester

M.

Sir John Riggs Miller, Bart. Dallington, 5 copies
Lady Riggs Miller, Ditto, 5 copies
Lady Musgrave, London
The Rev. M. Marcus, Northampton
Edward Morant Gale, Esq. Upton-House, 2 copies
Mrs. Morant Gale, Ditto, 2 copies
Brown Mostyn, Esq. Kiddington
Mrs. Brown Mostyn, Ditto
The Rev. William Mills, Magdalen-College, Oxford
Mrs. Mills, Deddington
John Mills, Esq. London
Mrs. Mills, London
Miss Mills, Ditto
Mrs. Martyn, Ladgershall-Rectory
Mrs. Manning, Deddington
Miss Manning, Ditto
Mrs. Marlin, Bloxham
Mrs. Manning, Croughton
Mrs. Morse, Neithorp-House
Mr. Joseph Montgomery, London
Mr. W. Manneville, Ditto
James Minn, Esq. Shouldern
Mrs. Minn, Ditto
Miss Malin, Brackley
Miss Milward, Banbury
Mrs. Munton, Ditto
Robert Mordaunt, Esq. Heythorp-Enstone
Charles B. Morgan, Esq. Daventry
The Rev. Charles Marsham, Caversfield
Sir Thomas Moystn, Bart. Swift's-House, 2 copies
The Rev. R. Mensham, St. Clements, Oxford
Mrs. Macbride, Oxford, 4 copies

N.

The Most Noble the Marquis of Northampton,
    Castle-Ashby
The Marchioness of Northampton, Ditto
Miss Nagle, Dallington
Miss Ann Nagle, Pengreep, Cornwall

The Rev. Thomas Nicholson
The Rev. T Nutt, Bodicott
George Nelson, Esq. Buckingham
Miss Elizabeth Nasbey, Banbury
Non mi recordo, Lake of Como

O.

Mr. Thomas O'Gery, Daventry
Miss Ormond, Bicester

P.

Sir Henry Peyton, Bart. Tusmore-House, 3 copies
Lady Peyton, Ditto, 2 copies
The Hon. P. S. Pierrepont, Evenly-Hall
The Hon. Mrs. Pierrepont, Ditto
Paynton Pigott, Esq. Bridge-Villa, Maidenhead
The Rev. R. Paine, Asprey, Bedfordshire
Mrs. R. Prettyman, Middleton-Stoney, 2 copies
Miss Peck, Oxford
Mr. Preedy, Bloxham
Richard Peyton, Esq. Birmingham
Miss E. F. Peyton, Ditto
Monsieur L'Abbe de la Porte, London
The Rev. John Prescott
Mrs. J. Palmer, Stratton-Audley
Miss Pearce, Stoney-Stratford
Mrs. Parker, Bicester
Mrs. Platford, Hull
Miss Paine, Banbury
Mr. Joseph Pain, Neithorp
Miss Paine, Ditto
Mrs. Pope, Abingdon
Mr. Page, Banbury
Mr. Perry, Sardon-School
Mrs. Perry, Shipston
Mr. Thomas Perry, Banbury
Mrs. Price, Deddington
Mrs. Philips, Montague-place, Russell-square, Lond
Robert Page, Esq. R. T. S. Madeira
Mr. B. W. Palmer, Daventry
The Rev. Mr. Pearson, Oxford
Mrs. Pillenger, Ditto
The Rev. William Perkins
Mrs. H. Parsons, Oxford

R

Archibald Robertson, M. D. Northampton
Mrs. Reanolds, 25, Bloomsbury-square, London
Mr. Rusher, Oxford
Mrs. Rann, Banbury
Mrs. Ross, London
Mrs. Rousby, Souldern
Mrs. Roots, Goddington
Miss Russel, Middleton-Cheney
Miss Reed, Hinton
Miss Rusher, Overthorpe
Mr. Thomas Rusher, Banbury
Mr. John Roberts, Ditto
Mr. A. Rutter, Ditto
Mrs. Mary Rose, Deddington
Miss Rebecca Root, Wardington
Mr. J. G. Rusher, Banbury

S.

The Rev. John Stoddart, Northampton
Christopher Smyth, Esq. Ditto, 3 copies
G. F. Stratton, Esq. Upper-Werton
———— Strickland, Esq. Cokethorpe-Park
Daniel Stewart, Esq. Wickham Park
Mrs. Stewart, Ditto
Mrs. Salmon, Hardwick-House
Richard Smith, Esq. Bicester
The Rev. Mr. Smalley, Banbury
The Rev. C. Smalley, Brailes
Miss Smalley, Ditto
T. Smallwood, Esq. Wilmorton
The Rev. R. S. Skillern, Chipping-Norton
Mrs. Smith, Charwelton
Miss Scott, Hinton
Miss S. Scott, Ditto
Mrs. Severne
Miss Severne
Miss Catherine Severne
Miss Solomon, Liverpool, 2 copies
Mrs. Smith, Deddington
Miss Spence, Culworth

c

William Stone, Esq. Buckingham
Mrs. Shouble, Bensington
Mrs. Edward Southam, Buckingham
Mr. H. Stilyres, Plumber's-Furze
Miss Sansbury, London
Mrs. Elizabeth Stone, Banbury
Mr. Lyne Spurrett, Ditto
Mrs. Staley, Ditto
Mr. Slater, Shelswell
Mr. C. Sharpe, Neithrop
Mrs. Stafford, Chacombe
Miss Snowe, Shipston
Miss Martha Sabin, Ditto
Mrs. Slatter, North-Aston
Mr. G. M. Smith, Chipping-Norton
Mrs. H. L. Smith, Southam
Mr. T. Sternberg, Northampton
Mrs. Smallbones, Hordley

T.

Sir George Throkmorton, Bart. Weston-Underwood
The Rev. Dr. Tatham, Oxford
The Rev. Francis Turville, Hampton
Miss Tubb, Bicester
The Rev. L. M. Turner, Bicester, 2 copies
William Tuckwell, Esq. Oxford
Mr. Charles Tomes, Jun. Ditto
Mrs. Taylor, Goddington-Hall
Miss Taylor, Ditto
The Rev. S. N. Taylor, Shipston
Thomas Tims, Esq. Banbury
Mrs. Tawney, Banbury, 2 copies
David Twopenny, Esq. Oriel College, Oxford
Mrs. Tanner, Goddington
Mr. W. Taylor, Jun. Finmere-Grange
Mrs. Taylor, Warkworth
Mrs. Turner, Hinton
Mrs. Tirpp, Brackley
Mr. Joshua Thorne, Banbury
Mr. John Turner, Epwell
Mr. Wm. Tibbetts, Brackley

V

Viscountess Newport
Mrs. Vincent, Oxford

W.

The Right Hon. Lord Willoughby de Broke
  Wellesbourne, 2 copies
Fiennes Wykham Marten, Esq. Leeds Castle, Maid-
  stone, Kent
The Rev. Charles Wetherell, Byfield Rectory
The Rev. John Whittenbury, Daventry
Dr. Williams, Regius Professor of Botany, in the
  University of Oxford
Dr. Wall, Oxford, 2 copies
Mrs. W. Walford, Banbury
Miss Wyatt, Ditto, 2 copies
Mrs. Theophilus Walford, Ditto, 2 copies
The Rev. T. Woodroofe, Drayton
Miss Walmersley, Hammersmith
Mrs. Woodman, Brackley-Rectory
Mrs. Robert Weston, Brackley
Mrs. Watson, Aynho
Mrs. Wells, Hornton
Thomas Williams, Esq. London
The Rev. Thomas Winter, Chipping-Norton
Benjamin Whitaker, Esq. London
Mrs. Whitaker, Ditto
Miss Wilson, Ditto
John Wilson, Esq. Adderbury
Mrs. Wagstaff, Windsor
Mrs. E. Winsor, London
Mr. Edward Wells, Woodstock
Miss Whitney, Buckingham
Mr. J. Wyatt, Banbury
Mr. John Williams, Adderbury
Mrs. Whetton, Banbury
E. W. Wright, Esq. Shipston
Mr. George Wells, Shipston
Miss Ward, Ditto
Mr. John George Walford, Banbury
Mr. M. Wilson, Ditto
Mr. Joseph Wells, Ditto

Mrs. Weston, Deddington
Miss Wells, Banbury
Mrs. Warriner, Bloxham-Grove
Rev. W. M. Whalley, Swarford
Mrs. Woolston, Adderbury
Mr. C. Whitton, Sulgrave
John Wardle, Esq. Wardington
The Rev. George Wasey, Ditto
Mr. J. Whitton, Sulgrave
Mr. Watson, Coton
Mrs. Windham, Charlotte-street, Bloomsbury-square
Mr. M. Wilson, Banbury
Miss Wood, Southam
J. M. Wardle, Esq. Daventry
Henry Walford, Esq. Bicester
R. Wootton, Esq. Oxford
The Rev. Dr. Winstanly, Albion-Hall, Oxford
Mr. Wade, Oxford
Mrs. Wheeler, Ditto

578 copies

MEMOIRS.

&c.

Various are the reasons which have induced me to write these Memoirs, which are compiled partly from authentic documents left by my deceased parent, who had collected many interesting anecdotes relative to our family, with such particular accounts of my ancestors, as were before unknown to me. I conceived it would be an agreeable employment of my leisure moments, to select and arrange from these papers, such material information as might be necessary for the completion of my narrative; but what outweighed every other consideration was, in my estimation, the liberal and candid way in which my father has faithfully delineated every minute circumstance, neither concealing any thing, or exaggerating in the least degree, but exhibiting only a true picture of events just as they occurred.

There are also other considerations which prompted me to this undertaking, and which I shall fully state. From the bosom of affluence, my family has been, in consequence of the French Revolution, reduced to comparative

B

indigence and obscurity : indeed what has not
this tremendous Revolution destroyed ? it has
inflicted the most fiery ordeal that any country
ever underwent ; and many, many years must
necessarily elapse, to heal the wounds, and
repair the ravages committed during its reign
of terror. Necessity therefore, and an anxious
desire to discharge some arrears of accompts,
due on my part ; and which the small pension
I receive from the French Government, is inadequate to meet, are the principal motives to
the publication of these Memoirs. The only
merit to which I aspire is, that of veracity in
the narration of my history; and the only apology
I can offer for my appearance in public is, the
desire of complying with the wishes of many
of my kindest friends. From my imperfect
knowledge of the English language, should
any inaccuracies have escaped my notice, I trust
they will be excused ; and as my motives are
pure, I repose with confidence on the liberality
of my readers. I proceed therefore to the
history of my ancestors, which I shall deliver
as nearly as possible in the words of my
deceased parent.

The Baron de K....., son of Louis Baron de
K....., was born on an estate belonging to his
father, in a town situate about .... leagues from
the river R...., in Germany. Being an only
son, and the family of Louis Baron de K.....,
one of the most ancient Baronial families of the
empire, as also a member of the circle of Bas
Rhin*, he was naturally obliged by his father

* Germany was formerly divided into nine great divisions,
called circles.—*Bas-Rhin*, or Lower Rhine, was one of the
three middle circles.

to enter into the service of a powerful monarch, who was engaged in frequent wars. This monarch, whom he served with great eclat, having no other object in view than the acquirement of honour and glory, and being by his fortune placed above necessity, he conferred credit on the different stations he held, without being obliged to sustain their splendour from the bounty of his prince, and as such he was at all times regarded, rather as a friend than as a servant. Ever frank and disinterested, if he did avail himself of the favors conferred on him by his priuce, it was solely that he might benefit others.

He entered the service of the prince of H. D.... as cadet in the guards of his Serene Highness; but he was soon after promoted gentleman of the chamber, and officer in the guards. The Prince was highly flattered, in having in his service the only son of the Baron de K....., so much so, that he acknowledged by his continued kindness towards the Baron, the high approbation he entertained for his son's assiduity in the diligent discharge of his duties. Although very young, he possessed the entire confidence of his master, and never did he meet with a denial in any thing he requested of him : of this, the following circumstance is a proof.

Two grenadiers of the guards one day deserted : as soon as their absence was discovered, his Royal Highness sent hussars, subalterns, and even officers, on the different roads to intercept them. My ancestor, although only seventeen years of age, but ever jealous of shewing himself worthy the favors of his prince, and attending only to the voice of glory, having disguised himself in his shooting dress, and taken with him the necessary instruments of authority, to make himself known in case of need, as officer of the Prince's guard, immediately departed, accompanied only by his dog, armed with a hanger and a double-barrelled gun ready loaded. He proceeded on the road which he imagined these deserters had taken : he travelled over a considerable extent of country without hearing any tidings of them ; at length he arrived at a mill, which was at no considerable distance from a neighbouring village : here he made enquiries relative to the objects of his search : and was apprised that they had actually not long since passed through to reach the neighbouring village, which was bordered on the frontiers of the Duchy of D......

Upon this information he continued his pursuit, but being extremely fatigued, he determined before he went to the Bailiff, to whom he intended paying a visit, upon taking some refreshment, and for this purpose he entered an inn on the road side. What then must have been his astonishment, when on entering this house he found the objects of his search, the two deserters quietly seated at table eating a piece of bread each, and drinking some beer, to recruit their strength to enable them to reach the frontiers, which sheltered them from all farther pursuit. These men, no doubt, already anticipated their safe arrival, since the place where they were detected, was very distant from the usual route generally taken by deserters : and it was by

mere accident only, they were discovered in
this place, where they must have believed they
had no longer any thing to fear. It is not
easily imagined with what terror these two men
were seized, when my ancestor, who although
only a youth, proved to be an officer, and
produced the necessary power to arrest them,
in order to have them conveyed in safety to
the garrison; and when, without being in the
least intimidated by their gigantic size,
said to them in a tone of authority, " You
are my prisoners, empty your pot of beer,
and we shall depart; in the mean time I
shall take some refreshment also." They
thus finished their beer, and asked permission
to have another pot brought in, which he
granted; but when that was emptied, and he
on his part had finished his frugal repast, and
they requested permission to have a third
supply, he resolutely refused. This astonished
them not a little, for they imagined it would be
easy for them to amuse a youth, until a favorable opportunity should occur to enable them to
evade or deceive him, and make their escape:
but the manner in which he refused their
demand, convinced them they had only to
obey; so that they proceeded on their road.
As soon, therefore, as they had left the house,
and entered a narrow valley, bounded on one
side by a frightful precipice, and on the other
by a sterile and craggy mountain, such as
the boldest man would not have ventured to
have climed, having directed them to walk
before him, he said, " Grenadiers, I command
you to march twenty-eight paces in advance of
me, and if you deviate from the road, (which

was almost impossible,) I swear that I will fire on you, and the same if you turn back against me."——They heard this command with coolness, and executed it without uttering a word : he on his part, put his double-barrelled gun, which was loaded, on his shoulder, and followed their steps.

Having travelled a league without any obstacle, the two Grenadiers now turned round towards him, threw themselves on their knees, and earnestly intreated him not to take them any farther ; and if pity for their sufferings did not engage him to give them their liberty, that he would kill them, rather than compel them to go to the garrison ; but he was deaf to their supplication, for he could not do it, without betraying his duty, which a gentleman could not do without dishonouring himself, at least he conceived so ; but on such an occasion it is necessary to possess much firmness of mind, not to be led away by the first impulse of the mind, which is that of pity : for a true gentleman, who has always in retrospect the actions of his illustrious ancestors, will never be guilty of a mean action ; for if in the first instance their virtue becomes a title for us, ours, if we follow their steps, adds an additional palm of glory to theirs ; which prevents the commission of any action which may render us unworthy of them.

At this moment how dreadful was the remorse of conscience in these defaulters, no means, no authority could stifle it : he, however, could not grant their earnest request ; he endeavoured to pursuade them with mildness to pursue their route, and boldly to face the danger which they dreaded; he assured them that they would have every indulgence to expect from the clemency of the prince, (who though certainly was not very lenient when military discipline was in question,) might be entreated in their favour, nor could these miserable men scarcely hope to escape punishment; such severe corporeal punishment, as appeared to them a thousand times worse than death itself. He at length prevailed upon them in making them continue their route, but when they had reached within about half a league of the town, the punishment which they expected so soon to endure, in an instant rushed on their minds in all its horrors: they sunk under the bare idea of submitting to it, in so short a time.—It being their first offence, they again threw themselves on their knees, and entreated him to take their lives, rather than compel them to proceed any farther; saying, at the same time, he was at liberty to do with them what he pleased, but that no human power should make them advance another step, unless they were dragged by main force.—All was of no avail, even his entreaties and kind persuasions had no effect on their obduracy. What then could a youth of his age do, without assistance in an open country, and himself too weak to compel them by force? One method only remained untried, but he was too high minded to have recourse to illusion, in promising them their pardon: for had he given his word of honour (which to him was sacred) and the prince should have refused to ratify it, he would be equally dishonoured. What

8

could be done? his entreaties and remonstrances were useless; but still he had hopes of influencing the Prince in their behalf, who was very partial to his soldiers, particularly so to the fine tall men, and as one of these deserters was the finest man in the whole company.

He then called him aside, and said, "Grenadier, you know the Prince sometimes honours me with his favour, I give you my word of honour that I will use all my interest with him to obtain your free pardon, if you will allow yourselves to be peaceably conducted to the castle, and instead of putting you in prison, which is the usual method on such occasions; I will take you to him, and in your presence render an account, with what mildness you permitted yourselves to be conducted hither, and I shall describe to him the repentance and remorse that has already penetrated your consciences, and be assured he will not refuse me your pardon." Encouraged by this discourse, which seemed to convey a salutary balm to their minds, they arose, and agreed to pursue their route. All the officers they afterwards met, complimented him on his success: but they were inwardly vexed that a youth should accomplish an action, which the boldest amongst them would not have attempted alone. And what, moreover, was their astonishment, when they saw him conduct his prisoners to the castle, instead of putting them under a military guard at the entrance; which they expected.

Thus a sudden ray of hope flashed on their

minds; but they trembled when he consigned them to the officer on guard at the anti-chamber, and was announced to the prince as being there with the two deserters.

The Prince instead of calling him to his presence, commanded the officer on guard to have them put in irons, saying, he would make a severe example of them on the morrow.

After giving some commissions to my ancestor, the Prince returned into his apartment, whilst my ancestor remained as though struck dumb with astonishment at the anger of his highness; yet his presence of mind did not wholly desert him: he followed the steps of the Prince, and placed himself unperceived by him, behind his chair, for the Prince always eat alone. Soon after, the Prince perceived some one behind his chair, he turned round, and seeing my ancestor, asked him his reasons for being there, saying, I shall take care of you, my child: you have performed an action, which deserves to be well recompensed, therefore rely upon me, and it shall be done; and I shall write to your father;—but as you must be much fatigued, go and rest yourself, and to-morrow you shall make your report to me. Perceiving the Prince was appeased, he threw himself at his feet, and said, if your Royal Highness thinks I merit a reward, permit me to request a favour. What, my child, would you wish me to do for you? said he, with heartfelt kindness; it is to order the removal of the irons from those two unfortunate men I have made prisoners, and be assured, your Highness, for the future they will be the more faithful in your service, and that if they had a thousand lives, they would sacrifice them for you. He then entered into a relation of the circumstances of their capture, and above all, dwelt on their having twice, on their return to the garrison, requested him to take their lives, rather than conduct them back to their just punition; at the same time stating, that he had given them his word of honour, to use every means in his power to soften the just wrath of their Sovereign. Besides, said he, if these mens' heart had been hardened in crime, it is certain my weakness must have sunk under their efforts to escape.

The Prince, softened and much affected by the generosity and courage of my ancestor, said to him, " Well, my child, go; I give up those two prisoners to you. I disengage you from your parole, and tell them it is to your intercession they owe their liberty; and further, order that meat and drink be given them at the office; but tell them, also, that in grant. ing them their pardon, 1 have made you responsible for their future conduct. And to enable you to watch over them more effectually, I give you the company of ...... in my guards, vacant by the dismission of Mr. ....

My ancestor embraced the knees of his Prince, and immediately flew to the place where these miserable men were confined. They were plunged into the most profound sorrow; expecting only to leave their dungeon at the fatal moment when they should be summoned to receive their merited punishment: but what were their emotions of joy, in seeing

him arrive. who, but a moment before, they
thought was the author of their misery, now
came as their liberator.

He said, "Arise, my children; by command
of the Prince, I come to relieve you from your
fetters, you are free, and for the future you are
my soldiers: your pardon only did I solicit, as
a recompence for my zeal in the service of my
sovereign; but he, always magnanimous and
generous, has by an excess of kindness, made
me your captain."

Who can paint the sensations these miserable
men experienced, in embracing the knees of
their benevolent liberator and captain; they
swore in the enthusiasm of their joy, a thousand
and a thousand times over, that they would be
ever faithful to the commands of such a captain.

He raised them himself from the ground, and
gave orders at the office to provide these men
with food, which was immediately done.

Thus the soldiers, women, and children, all
gave him a thousand blessings.—What can be
put in competition with the exquisite feelings of
a virtuous mind; conscious of its having accomplished a meritorious action, no pleasure
can vie with these feelings of self complacency,
which are often more pleasing than all the
praise that may be lavished by a numerous
public; and since nothing could sully such
pure motives, who could wish for more?
cherished as he was by his prince, respected
and beloved by all around him, unless it were
to have for a partner a sensible and faithful
woman?

The moment was not far distant! A short time
after the occurrence which I have related, the
Princess was delivered of a son, who was named
Frederick; on this occasion, my ancestor was
chosen by his master, to carry the news of the
birth of a son to the Prince's father, who was
then Sovereign Prince, residing in the capital at
L....t, at D..... He immediately departed
as courier with his despatches, and arrived at
D....., where he learnt that his Highness was
distant some leagues from home, on a hunting
excursion with a whole retinue, in the large
forest, and was not expected to return for some
days.—In consequence of this information, he
made for the hunting lodge of the prince, but
did not find him there, as his Highness was
already in the hunt.

As it may not be unacceptable to my readers
to have described to them the manner in which
the grand hunt is conducted in Germany, I will
endeavour briefly to relate it. When the
Prince proposes a grand hunt,* he commands
his huntsman, who is always commandant of
the guard and chamberlain, to make the necessary preparations. This huntsman, who is
usually stiled (the *Yieger Meister*,) causes
several thousand peasants to be assembled, and
orders them to form a large circle round the
forest, each peasant taking his proper post.
His subalterns then give a signal, by sounding
their horns; when all of them are instantly
required to advance in regular order, and at
the same time to make a great shout: at this

* A grand hunt is not a very frequent entertainment in
Germany, it is generally resorted to upon some great
festival, or signal occasion.

noise the stags, hinds, wild boars, and all the beasts take immediately to their flight, in order that they may shelter themselves in the interior of the woods; at the end of a few days, the circle is very considerably diminished, and all the animals, are, as it were, confined within its limits. When the circle is sufficiently diminished, the whole circumference is well staked round, and secured with cords, made for this purpose, very strong, and placed sufficiently high, so that none of the beasts may escape, and a guard stationed on the exterior to add to these means of detention! During the interval taken up in these necessary precautions, which generally occupy a considerable space of time, an amphitheatre is erected under a canopy, which is so raised from the ground, as to prevent any danger to the occupants, with respect to the wild beasts, who are most cruelly tormented, as will be seen in the sequel.

The Prince is stationed on this amphitheatre, with his suit; and behind the ring of cords are placed the chariots, from of which the operations of the chace are performed. They then first separate the wild deer, which are to be preserved alive, from the rest of the herd, and send them to the Prince's park. Those who are to assist in the hunt, are placed in these chariots, a considerable number of which being reserved for the nobility of the city and neighbourhood, who are always present on these occasions.

'The day the grand hunt begins, the Prince places himself under the canopy, and from

thence selects those animals which he wishes
to have preserved for his park; these are soon
taken in nets, made for this purpose. The
Prince then commences the hunt, by darting a
kind of tubular fire arrow, which penetrates
the skin and flesh of the wild boars, and immediately sets fire to and burns them. These
tortured animals, of course, strive in every
possible way to disengage themselves from the
shafts; but no sooner are any of these arrows
extinguished, ere fresh ones are darted upon
them, until it is the Prince's pleasure to forbear
these horrid tortures; which very often does
not take place, until actual fatigue unfits them
for the contest, and obliges them to desist.
The Prince then commands them to be slain,
and sometimes kills them himself. After having thus most dreadfully tortured the wild
boars, in this extremely cruel manner, the
Prince farther commands the circle to be
diminished; the butchery then begins : stags,
hinds, wild boars, &c. &c. are killed with the
carbines, until but few escape, on account of
their distance : not only does the Prince fire,
but also those of the court who are invited,
and served with carbines by his Highness;
which is considered a great honour. After
having killed some hundreds of all kinds, ca-
valiers from the nobility, or the court, enter
the circle on foot, to defy the wild boars to
personal combat, which is effected in the following manner. The hunter is armed with his
hanger, and is surrounded by his pikes for
safety, in case the wild boar should overthrow
him, to be enabled at the instant, to secure
assistance; he then takes his hanger by the

hilt, places it on his knee, and thus irritates the wild boar with the point of its blade. The boar seldom fails rushing furiously open mouthed on his antagonist; and then the hunter, after having shewn his dexterity, and for some time wearied the ferocious creature, plunges the hanger down its throat, into the heart of the animal. After this spectacle is finished, the hunters from the common class destroy, in their turn, with their carbines, a number of smaller boars; after which, the circle of ropes is removed, to give liberty to those animals that have escaped the carnage, or that are not so dreadfully wounded, as to cause their death.

It was on an occasion like this which I have now described, that my ancestor found the then reigning Prince of D..... Having been announced to his Highness, he was introduced into the pavilion, where he delivered his despatches to the Prince, who was so much pleased with his message, that he immediately conferred upon him very marked attention and kindness, and at once commanded the Baron de N.....h to present him with a carbine, to take part in the hunt.

After the termination of this scene, my ancestor returned with the court to the hunting lodge of the Prince, who granted him permission to ride in his carriage, with himself and chamberlain. While travelling, the Prince said to the Baron de N.....h, (for he he was always his favorite,) " Attend, here is a fine youth; (speaking of my ancestor,) I am resolved he shall marry thy Caroline. What say you, young gentleman, I assure you she is a genteel girl." The Baron de N.... replied, "as it pleases your Royal Highness, if the young man is agreeable, and is approved by my daughter, I shall not object." Then said the Prince, "as soon as we arrive, give orders that fresh relays of horses be provided ; and as A.... is not very distant, we will proceed thither, for we must know if she is agreeable to the match" Addressing himself again to my ancestor, he asked, if he gave his consent : he replied, "whatever your Royal Highness chooses, will be highly agreeable to me, but as my dependance rests on two persons, whose consent is indispensable, the one, his Highness your son, the latter my father." This, said the Prince, I will take upon myself ; I will send one of my gentlemen to my son, to announce your arrival here, and by him make the demand in your name, and I am certain he will not refuse me : as to what relates to the other person, who is your father, as soon as you have seen your intended, you shall go to him yourself, and carry my request. Here the subject closed, and the interview finished.

When princes meddle in matrimonial connections, it is very rare that parents oppose ; in this case, moreover, nothing derogatory to the family of the Baron de N.....h, which was as ancient as our own, could be urged. The gentleman therefore, who was despatched by the Prince, having soon arrived with the consent of his son, my ancestor was sent home, bearing the request of the Prince, and to obtain his father's permission ; and two days after his return, the marriage was celebrated, under the most flattering auspices; but I shall be silent on the happiness of this union.

After his marriage, my ancestor departed with his amiable wife, to attend the Prince his master; who, on her arrival, was made maid of honour to the Princess: indeed, both of them had places at court, and were allowed peculiar privileges. But my ancestor having so very young a wife, who was only fourteen years of age when married, felt too jealous of such juvenile charms, to remain very long at court, and therefore, in spite of all its gaiety, and the pleasures which it afforded, it soon became wearisome to him; he consequently solicited his dismissal, which, however, was as constantly refused.

A short time after my ancestor's nuptials, his father died: new pretexts were accordingly presented, to obtain his dismission from the palace; such, that as his mother was left a widow, with a family, her domestic affairs would require to be arranged by him. But though his entire dismissal from court was objected to, he was yet offered leave of absence for a short time, which he accepted: and at the expiration of this period, being recalled by the Prince, he arrived at court, leaving his wife with his mother; on his return, he again solicited his dismission, which at length he obtained, and most certainly under very flattering conditions.

The Prince said to him, I grant you your dismission as captain of the guards, but not as gentleman of the chamber; and I farther require your presence every year, to spend

C

three months with me, not on duty, but as a companion and friend.

My ancestor's accustomed disinterestedness prevented his retaining the emolument which was offered him, from his vacated situation in the guards ; he thought too nobly, to receive emolument without performing his duty; he therefore declined accepting it.

It is true, that during his stay at court, he was at no expence on his own account, being accommodated with his suite, at the Prince's own cost. Yet the charges of travelling were not very inconsiderable, and would have afforded a reasonable plea for retaining his pay.

Besides, soon after his retirement from the court, his wife had the misfortune to lose her father, who, in consequence of an accident arising from the overthrow of his carriage whilst he was in it, and which was simply occasioned by his horses taking fright at a stag, which unexpectedly darted from a wood, while pursued by the hounds and the huntsmen, directly in front of them, died so suddenly, that he made no settlement upon his daughter. She was therefore left without dowry ; and although her sister, married to the Baron D......g, had her portion of his property, yet it became necessary to wait until the death of her mother, which happened in the year 17..

After my ancestor, therefore, had received his dismission, he retired to his estate at G.... where my father was born ; in order that he might himself assist in the management of his estate, since it required the greatest economy to support the ancient dignity of his house; which though formerly one of the most affluent, at that time was gradually decaying, and in consequence of accumulated misfortunes and losses, was greatly on the decline. One principal cause to which this change of affairs may be attributed, was the war carried on against this country by the French, who took every thing and spared nothing. This family, besides, had to indemnify the farmers, and others, who had likewise been injured by the war; it was sufficient for such persons to have been unfortunate, to have had a claim on the munificence of their superiors. But though assistance was furnished, merely by way of loan, yet these loans were never repaid; and among the number were the inhabitants of one whole village. Loans were also granted to the county of L....ges...y and M...heim: for the recovery of which, from these two places, my family pleaded a very long time, at the chamber of W...... This almost ruined them with law expences: for after they had gained the process, if it can be called gaining a cause when one is obliged to pay expences, and content oneself with only one half of one's property, my ancestor himself was compelled to borrow considerable sums upon his estate, &c.

I shall now proceed to lay before my readers, an account of the life of my father, from which I have wandered, in order that I might furnish them with some information respecting the family of De Poly in general. It will be more easy, however, after this digression, to form a better judgment of what follows.

The life of my father, as will be seen in the sequel, has been a tissue or series of blessings and misfortunes. He proceeded in his career without any fixed plan, similar to a vessel bereft of all its sails, while navigating a stormy sea ; yet, at the same time, the invisible hand of divine Providence, which incessantly directs our destiny, and which alone can regulate it, never deserted him. Thus was he circumstanced at the age of twenty six : his youth was impetuous, and full of storms ; he therefore attached himself to every chimerical ray of hope, so much so, that the extreme vivacity of his natural disposition, and an ardent desire of arriving the soonest at the object, whatever it might be, which he had in view, led him to consider every shadow as a reality ; but this delusion was only of short duration.

At an early age, he was placed under the care of a private tutor, and under the more immediate eye of his grandmother (on the father's side) and aunt, who conjointly with his ecclesiastical preceptor, impressed on his mind the sacred and wise precepts of religion, without the observance of which, no permanent happiness can be expected in this life, or in that which is to come. They frequently exhorted him to have the fear of God always before his eyes ; and assured him that it is religion which instructs us in every necessary duty, and will be our consolation in the time of distress and misfortune.

At the age of twelve years, he was sent to college, in the city of G. . . . .t, which was but a small distance from the Count of L. . . . .ges, into the which he was admitted, on account of his high birth.

He possessed much influence with the old Countess, the widow of the late reigning Count ; this lady was extremely devout, and frequently made prayers and lectures to him, as did also the Baroness de B...., with whom he was likewise in favour. The days spent in the society of these ladies were very agreeable to him ; for although he was but young, and extremely vivacious, he yet seldom joined his companions in their amusements at the college. My father was naturally very generous, and when he had money, it was not unfrequently given to the first comers, who might be in want ; especially to French soldiers, whom he knew by their uniforms. But his greatest *fort* was for horses and equestrian exercises. He endeavoured also to acquire some knowledge of the mechanical arts, &c. and for this purpose, he traversed the city of G...... repeatedly, and visited manufactories of every kind. He examined into every trade and profession, from the cordwainer's stall, to the painter's chamber ; but without acquiring a competent knowledge of either, he contented himself with merely questioning the workmen, &c. in their various employments. For chemistry, certainly, he had a great partiality, and to it he therefore applied himself strenuously, as will be seen hereafter.

My father was originally destined for the church ; but the army had much greater allurements for him. One day, while jesting with his companions, one of them seized him, and threw him down on a rugged stone; he instantly felt his knee much hurt, and immediately called out for assistance : they helped him up, but he could not stand ; they were, therefore, obliged to carry him to his room, and put him to bed. A physician was procured without delay, who said there was no fracture, and ordered the knee to be rubbed with spirits, &c. and a strengthening plaster to be applied round it ; but his knee swelled more and more, to such a degree, that the Rector deemed it necessary to acquaint his family with the circumstance : who, ou receipt of this information, were much alarmed, and immediately sent servants with their carriage for him, G...t being only seven leagues distant. On his arrival at home, the most celebrated physicians were sent for, who also assured his parents that no bone was fractured. The swelling and inflammation, however, continued the same, in spite of all the remedies applied ; nor could he stand, or bear ever so lightly on that leg, without pain. For nearly twelve months, he remained, under the care of these celebrated, but ignorant disciples of Æsculapius ; being the whole of this time generally obliged to rest his leg on a sofa or bed. At length a country physician arrived, who had resided a considerable time in England, who never until that time, had the honour to prescribe in the family ; but finding the most celebrated men could do no good, and that this person requested permission to see my father ; his request was complied with. As soon as he had carefully examined the knee, he declared there was a fracture, and offered to undertake the cure, which was at once agreed to ; and thus in consequence of this gentleman's great skill, and new mode of treatment, in the course of a month my father was enabled to bear on his leg, and even to walk a little; and in a few weeks he quite recovered from his lameness.

Sometime after my father's recovery, my grandfather, De Poly, proposed to him the choice of his profession, the church or the army. To the latter he gave his decided preference. "Well," said his father, "since you have made choice of the army, I will present you to his Highness L...... de D....., my old master, who has become, since the death of his father, Landgrave; and who will, most assuredly, on account of the friendship subsisting between us, take every care of you, if you conduct yourself in a proper manner to merit his kindness." But my father, who had a much greater inclination for the French service, frankly said, perhaps a little too abruptly, "No, no, I will never serve with such soldiers, but I shall be most happy to serve his Majesty the king of France."

His father, extremely angry at the contempt shewn by his son, at those troops in the which he had himself served for many years, said to him in an ironical manner, "Yes, yes, you shall serve his most Christian Majesty, by my sending you to the place of confinement at M....., where you will receive ninety lashes of the whip, and be compelled to salute the door-sill on your entrance." My father was but little disturbed by this menace, for he well knew his father's fondness for him. Some days, however, passed without his hearing any

thing more on this subject, till at length
his father, without the least appearance of
anger, proposed an excursion, which was
highly pleasing to him, and to which he
assented ; being, as was before observed, very
fond of equestrian exercise. On the road,
according to custom, he had a lecture, on the
folly of his choice, enforcing the necessity of
his compliance with his father's wishes ;
reminding him of the great kindnesses he had
formerly received from the Prince, and the
advantages and sudden promotion naturally to
be expected in his service, rather than in the
one he had chosen. And, moreover, that his
father's old master would, without doubt, heap
favours on him ; and if his conduct merited it,
would be his friend : besides, that he would in
this service be benefited by the advice of his
father's old friends, some of whom he had left
at court, and others in the different regiments
in the service. But deaf to all his father's
arguments, he attended only to what suited his
own inclination ; that is to say, his entering
into the service of his most Christian Majesty,
the king of France. His father perceiving that
he could gain no ascendancy over him, although he was inwardly much displeased with
him, did not at this time let him discover his
disappointment, which his son considered as a
favourable omen.

About eight days after this conversation, one
evening his father said to him, "My son, will you
accompany me to-morrow morning to W . . . . .
(a town a few leagues distant from his father's
residence,) knowing at the same time that his
son's partiality for travelling, would prevent

a refusal; for that though he was not so
fond of riding in a coach, as on horseback,
yet the pleasure of travelling with his father,
whom he at all times almost adored, would,
notwithstanding his severity, prompt his compliance.

' On the following morning the Berlin was
brought to the door, and they were informed
the carriage was ready; it being very early,
before break of day, and still quite dark, the
servants were provided with flambeaux, to
enable them to make the necessary arrangements. By this light, my father perceived a
large trunk, fastened to the back of the Berlin,
which made him start with fear, lest there
should be some scheme in this journey; and
made him conjecture, that perhaps his father
might intend to take him into confinement at
M.,....; and the more so, since the high
road to W.... led to it. But if such had
been his father's intention, he had no means
of preventing it; they therefore got into the
carriage, accompanied by a valet de chambre,
and the necessary servants to escort them.

When they arrived at W......, his father
alighted, and paid some visits to his friends
who resided there, leaving orders to have the
horses refreshed during his absence. On his
return, they again proceeded on their journey;
but instead of returning homeward, they took
the road to M...... This greatly terrified
my father, yet he dared not say any thing, or
even let his alarm be perceived; at length
they arrived at the very place which occasioned
all his fears, nor is it easy to conceive his

agonized feelings at the moment which, although groundless, were yet not less painful.

They were driven to the best hotel in the town, supper was ordered, and there they slept. But before they went to bed, his father had occasion to go into the town; during his absence, therefore, his son endeavoured to learn from the valet de chambre, their destination; but every thing seemed enveloped in the deepest mystery, and he could gain no information from this person, to satisfy his curiosity. After some length of time, his father returned, and ordered the carriage to be ready early in the morning.

The miserable night my father passed in this gloomy uncertainty, will be readily conceived; at break of day, however, they were summoned, the carriage being ready, and they departed from this much dreaded place, and travelled the whole of the day, until at night they alighted at a small town.

Here my father was almost transported with joy, when he discovered the *fleurs de lis* on the uniforms of the soldiers; which at once flashed conviction on his mind, that they were already in the French territory; and all his glory seemed to concentrate, in his being permitted to serve the great monarch of France.

After he had made this discovery, he threw himself at the feet of his father, and embraced his knees, which he moistened with his tears; but not tears of fear, such as escaped him in the town of M . . . . . ., but tears of joy and gratitude. His astonished father exclaimed, " what means all this, my son ?"   " Ah ! best of fathers, ever kind parent," he replied, "I am at the summit of my most ardent hopes; we are in France." He was asked, how he knew that he was in France: "there are," said he, "the well known *fleurs de lis* on the uniforms of all the soldiers; this plainly tells me that I am in France." His father, finding it useless longer to endeavour to conceal his design, said, "Well, my son, I am taking you to the regiment of H......, D....st, in the service of the king of France, who is the son of my master our Prince, and who is *Commandant*. He is at present, I believe, at L....., where we shall arrive in about four days. I shall then place on you, for the first time, the uniform you have been so anxious to wear; and you will then be in the service of a king whom you love, without your having ever seen him. What can be the infatuation which inclines you rather towards him, than any other of the great potentates, whose different uniforms you have seen?"

It was an inward prepossession which prompted my father to give this preference to the king of France.

At the expiration of the four days, they arrived at St......., whence they expected to find the regiment of Hesse Darmstadt, but did not, it being in garrison at S..... L.....; a very unhealthy situation.

His father, therefore, alarmed for his son's health, made choice of the regiment of D.....ce, of which, the Prince M..... de D...... was Colonel; and on the morrow took him to his Highness, whom he knew, from his having married a princess of the house of H...... D....st.

In presenting the youth, he said, "I bring your Highness, my son, who has objected to serve in the troops in which I served; and has declared he will serve none other than his Majesty the king, your master. For this reason, I request you will have the kindness to receive him into your regiment, as a common soldier; my will is, that he sleep in the same room with the other soldiers, take his meals with them, and that he be not exempted from any duty a soldier is obliged to perform; not even in the most trifling circumstance: for we must, before we arrive at command, learn to obey; which duty he has not yet been taught to put in practice." This language was, undoubtedly, very severe; the Prince, nevertheless, but very feebly opposed it, and said, "I receive him as the son of a gentleman, and as a volunteer into my regiment; he shall be lodged according to your desire, in a public room, where he will sleep with the Serjeant Major of the company; and I shall place him in the company of the Baron de B....; Monsieur Klo.... who is Lieutenant Colonel, will be his master; and the 2d Captain of the company, Monsieur D'ux......, he will have no higher pay than 2s. 6d. per day. And if, (said the Prince,) at the end of six months, he has acquired a perfect knowledge of his exercise, manœuvres, &c. he will be promoted."

All this perfectly coincided with the wishes of his father: who, although well pleased thus to punish him, for refusing to enter into the service of L.... de H.... D....; yet was unwilling that his son should continue too long a private soldier.

The Prince then ordered Mons. Klo.., Lieut. Colonel, to be called into his presence, and said, " I place this young gentleman under your direction, watch over his conduct; and you are required to make the necessary arrangements for his reception in your company."

After receiving the Prince's commands, the Lieut. Colonel retired. His father then remained in private conversation, in the Prince's apartment. After which, having taken leave, the Serjt. Major was sent for, to the hotel : he was a man of tolerable good physiognomy, excepting a monstrous pair of mustaches, which gave an appearance of ferocity, not very pleasing at first sight to a timid young man. He was invited to supper, which he accepted; after which, my father went with him to the muster, and the same evening was installed into the chamber and bed of this said Serjt. Major.

The following morning they called at the hotel, and dined with his father ; but it was for the last time, although he remained some days in the town, for the purpose of seeing how his son would accustom himself to this new mode of life. Some money having been given to him, he treated his comrades of the chamber, and several subaltern officers, and other soldiers of the regiment, with beer, &c.

Although he slept with the Serjt. Major, yet my father was not permitted to dine alone, as he did. He was, however, after some little time, allowed occasionally to dine in the town, at a friend's house:

On the day after his arrival, the tailor of the regiment took his measure, to equip him from head to foot in his new regimentals, which were ordered to be made precisely of the same cloth as those of the private soldiers ; excepting only a narrow silver lace, which was to be put round the collar of his uniform, to distinguish him from the other soldiers : which was the only mark of distinction then in vogue, by which those of high birth were recognized.

When thus accoutred, he was presented by the Serjt. Major to his Captains, and by one of them to the Prince, who received him with great kindness ; recommending him to conduct himself well, to learn his discipline and manœuvres perfectly, that he might be in time advanced to the rank of officer ; apprised him that if he should fail in his duty, the Serjt. Major was to render an account to his Captain, who would order him under arrest ; and that if he committed faults of greater importance, they were to render an account to him personally, that he himself might order his confinement in prison: but no one was to be allowed to strike him ; at which, my father was much surprised ; yet such were the commands of the Prince.

But although my father was only a private, he was regarded by his comrades not only as a gentleman, but as an officer.

Notwithstanding these restrictions and in-junctions of the Prince, none of which, my father had ever himself violated, great was his astonishment sometime after, to see the Serjt. Major arrive, and take away his old clothes, to sell them, to prevent any of the

other soldiers making use of them, to facilitate
their desertion : who at the same time offered
him some money ; saying, " take this, it is your
enlisting money." " What!" said my father,
" enlisting money!—can it be possible?"—He
refused, moreover, to receive it ; the Prince having, so short a time before, given him to understand that he had not enlisted, but volunteered.
"It is, nevertheless," said the Serjt. Major, " by
the Prince's order, and without complying with it
you cannot remain in the regiment." " Very
well," said my father, " keep this money, and in
the mean time I will speak to the Captain about
it, and if necessary, to the Prince himself."
He accordingly went immediately to the Captain, but did not meet with him ; he then,
without hesitation, proceeded to the Prince
himself. Being admitted, he explained to his
Highness the purport of his visit : who replied
with kindness, " My child, it is expressly pro-
hibited to receive into the regiment, any person whomsoever, without his having contracted
an engagement by enlisting ; but of what
import is this? it is for form's sake only : and
it will not prevent or retard your promotion."

What, therefore, could my father do now,
being so far distant from home, and without
friends, of whom he could ask advice ?—He
was of necessity, obliged to obey the dictates
of the Prince : besides, suspicion never entered
his thoughts, and he would have committed
a kind of sacrilege, in supposing the Prince to
have been capable of artifice. The reader, however, will form his own opinion from the sequel.

My father, then, was only fourteen years of
age when he entered into the service, A. D. 1784.

The bounty money was accordingly taken; which, however, he considered as unworthy of him, being, as it were, the price of his person: on taking it, therefore, he immediately divided it among his comrades of the chamber, to whom it afforded a high treat. He then learnt his exercise; but not being strong enough to use a musket of the usual *calibre*, his mentor, the captain, lent him his; for at this period the officers had a very light musket, which they carried on parade, &c.

It being particularly wished, that my father should acquire the French language, a master was provided; but to no purpose, as he would not learn it. He was, therefore, required to assign his reasons, which were, that as the regiment was a German regiment, and they spoke and gave the word of command in the German language, (although in the service of France,) he was not inclined to learn the French tongue. Nor could they by any means persuade him to the contrary. He was accordingly ordered under personal arrest; and to make him the more ashamed, the Prince directed that he should be followed every where by a soldier of the chamber, with fixed bayonet.—But as all this was of no avail, after sometime had elapsed, he was released from his arrest, and the encumbrance of his unwelcome attendant, who was equally pleased by this decision. He applied himself, therefore, closely to his discipline, and learnt the different manœuvres with twelve men of the company, who were paid by his father, for this purpose.

My father had now mounted guard more than six months past, and the Prince, moreover,

every time he met him, said something flattering, and observed he should not forget him.
About this time, also, he received a letter from
his father, with the address of the Baron of
S...., his father's friend; and as there was
no fear of his deserting, he had the privilige
of the gates, the same as an officer; that is, by
the mark on his collar, he was permitted egress
and regress through the gates of the town,
which was not allowed the privates, without an
officer's permission. One day walking with
some subalterns, he met his cousin, who was
an officer in the regiment, and who appeared
not to notice him, owing to his being dressed
like a private; but it was not so when he wore
epaulettes; his cousin then thought himself
much honoured in his company, and moreover,
found the dinners and suppers given by his
relation, very good; which, it must be confessed, were not intended solely from friendship,
but more to gratify his own self-love.

My father's time passed pleasantly enough; and
as he could not keep his money for twenty four
hours together in his pocket, he gave it to
the soldiers in the regiment, or expended it
with his comrades of the chamber. After this
profuse and liberal distribution of his money,
he has been frequently obliged even to sell a
part of his allowance of bread, to purchase
hair powder for parade days, none being used
at other times, it being contrary to the regulations.

His military duty my father performed himself,
but he had a soldier to clean his accoutrements,
and mend for him, whom he paid for this
purpose. He sometimes, also, borrowed money

D

on his father's account, who had the kindness to discharge these sums regularly for him ; they were always, however, very small sums, and therefore deemed of little consequence.

My father, becoming ill of the Dysentery, was sent to the hospital, where he experienced the treatment of an officer, having a private room to himself; but he soon became tired of being alone. His father being informed of his son's illness, sent his own servant to attend him ; but as my father was well nursed, he ordered him to return back, and inform his friends, that every possible care was taken of him, and that his attendance was quite unnecessary. His recovery, however, was very slow ; but at length he was so far restored to health, as to be able to leave the hospital.

Soon after his recovery, he resumed his military duty; but as he had now been a private soldier for twelve months, he began to feel very impatient, and accordingly made complaints to his father about his not being promoted, and to the Baron of S....., who entertained the same opinion on the subject. His father, therefore, addressed a letter to the Prince, but received only evasive answers.

About this time arrived the regiment of H.... D.... of S.. L..., at St....., to join in the garrison of the place. His father, consequently, renewed his entreaties with his Colonel, who answered in the same evasive manner as before, and said it was impossible to advance him at that time. having had previous applications made to him, from his own relations, in order that he would forward the

interest and promotion of some young gentlemen, whom he could not discard; but that
my ancestor might rely on the first vacant place
that should occur, (after their advancement,)
being reserved for him.

His father now clearly perceived that there
was no intention of promoting his son, and
proceeded to the Prince his master, to request
a sub-lieutenancy for him; to which the Prince
readily consented: but at the same time,
required him to obtain the permission of his son,
who was Colonel *Commandant*, and with whom
he was not on the best terms. My ancestor
had much influence with this Prince, and
succeeded in accommodating their differences
before his departure, and was most happy to
carry this good news to his son: the dispute
originated merely in the too great lenity of
the son, on particular occasions.

It is due not only to truth, but that just
homage to which the virtues of these Princes
entitle them, to say they are as benevolent as they
are good, toward the unfortunate; naturally mild,
humane, and compassionate; distress had a
right to their kindness and liberality: always
hastening to prevent, if possible, or to alleviate
misery wherever it was known to them. Each
day they appeared in public was a holiday,
their sole presence seemed a benefit:—and by
how many other advantages was it not succeeded?

When they appeared in public, they were
followed by the blessings of the people, and
on those days was usually distributed, by their
order, to each necessitous individual, a certain
sum of money.

I must now return to my narrative. My ancestor had good news to communicate to the Prince Frederick; and on his arrival at St....., was accommodated at the Prince's hotel. He was accompanied by his sister, who had expressed a particular wish to see her nephew, whom she had not seen for a very long time.

On their arrival, a servant was sent to him, and to diminish his surprise, had orders to state that his father had just arrived with a friend, and that they were waiting for him at the Prince's hotel: he immediately followed the servant, and after traversing several apartments, had the felicity of finding, in a magnificent saloon, his father; when throwing himself on his knees, he raised him up and clasped him in his arms, where he remained some minutes, without either the one or the other being able to utter a word; but the natural impatience of his aunt did not permit her long to remain a silent spectatoress of so affecting a scene; nor can any express the joy and surprise he experienced at their sudden appearance. She overwhelmed him with the tenderest and most flattering epithets: he had always been the favorite of this lady.

What was now his happiness?—all his former hardships and sufferings vanished in an instant; he forgot his being a simple soldier, and was rejoiced to find himself still the beloved son and happy nephew.

After a short interval of silence, his father communicated to him the purport of his journey, and his expectations: that he had been announced to the Prince, (who was impatient to see him), and would do so as soon as he could disengage himself from his avocations. A message from the Prince was accordingly soon after communicated, through his valet de chambre, requesting his attendance, if the fatigue of his long journey would permit. His father instantly waited on his Highness, by whom he was most cordially received as the friend of his father. This good Prince granted my ancestor's request, and expressed himself much pleased in being able to oblige him; but felt sorrow he could not immediately receive his son into his regiment, no commission being vacant: but observed, that in the interim he would write to court for a commission, with an unlimited furlough; and farther, that he would allow him to remain with his parent, until called into actual service, and that he would request the permission of the Prince M.... the Colonel, to let him depart with them.

On the morrow, the Prince Frederick, accompanied by my grandfather, waited on the Colonel, but he refused to grant the son permission to leave his regiment; stating it to be his intention to promote him. But my ancestor, much incensed with him for his fallacious promises, and above all, being supported in his claim by the Prince Frederick, said undisguisedly, that he had already obtained the ratification from his master, and that the Prince F..... had agreed to receive him into his regiment, and he should no longer allow him to remain in the regiment of D..... The Colonel then declared my father was his soldier, and that he would not permit him to leave the regiment.

The Prince Frederick, very much displeased with this answer, exclaimed, " He is my officer, and although he may be your soldier, I shall know how to oblige you to give him up to me," and immediately left the room.

Soon after, a regular application was made at court; but in the mean time, my father was obliged to attend to his former duty as a private; though he invariably waited every day on his father at the hotel.

The time passed here so rapidly, that one day he absolutely forgot the hour of muster, until he heard the drums of the regiment of H.... D.... H.....; he then immediately ran to the barracks, quite out of breath, and was barely in time to answer to his name, which was then being called. At the end of fifteen days, however, his commission arrived, with the order to his Colonel to release him. He accordingly paid his respects to his new Colonel, the Prince Frederick, who command-ed his valet de chambre to have him equipped from top to toe in the regimentals of Hesse Darmstadt; after which, a place was taken for him in the coach, the money necessary to defray the expences of his journey given to him, with an unlimited leave of absence. He thus returned to his home, where he arrived in a few days, to the great satisfaction of his parents and friends. Here, for sometime, he amused himself in rural sports, and formed an acquaintance with a young surgeon, son of the Counsellor to the Duke of Wurtemberg, to whom he paid frequent visits, as also to other acquaintances in the neighbourhood.

My ancestor always treated his son with great kindness, without ever permitting the least appearance of disrespect; observing to him more than once, "if thou wert ever so great, even a Mareschal of France, it would not prevent me from correcting you, on the least shew of disrespect."—Such is the spirit of parents in Germany, which may appear strange here; but it has the good effect of producing the greatest respect from children towards their parents. In Germany, also, children are not exempt from saluting, morning and evening, the hands of their parents, and to ask their blessing before they leave home or retire to rest.

My father, who had two horses for his own use, generally paid his visits in the neighbourhood on foot, taking with him his servant, his dog, and gun, and shooting by the way for amusement. One day he paid a visit to his cousins, in the vintage month; and being much fatigued, he remained in bed the next morning later than usual; his aunt came to request him to rise and accompany her to the vineyards, where his cousins were already; but as he had passed a very restless night, and had no wish to comply, he said, he was inclined to have a little more sleep. His aunt insisted upon his rising, but he was equally obstinate in refusing. She became angry; this, however, did not prevent his remaining in bed: she, therefore, left him, saying, he should pay dearly for his obstinacy. After having sufficiently reposed himself, he arose, and immediately went to his cousins in the vineyards, where he found his dear aunt pouting: his cousins perceived it, and in

vain wished to find out the cause: for her self-
love was too much mortified by his refusal, to
admit of any explanation on his part, on the
subject.

At the hour of dinner, which was agrestic,
inasmuch as it consisted of a cold repast, which
the servants had brought with them from
home; it happened that his cousins asked the
servant for something, which, unfortunately,
had been forgotten; my father, therefore, from
gallantry on his part, (or perhaps some other
motive,) immediately ran as swiftly as possible,
and in a few minutes returned with it. This
trait of politeness was like a clap of thunder
to his aunt, who said to herself, see, he pays
more attention to the servant, than to me,
he must, undoubtedly, be in love with her.

My father little thought of the storm which
was now gathering over his head; he purposed,
moreover, making a week's stay with his
cousins, but at the end of three days, a servant
of his father's arrived, requesting his immediate return home. It was already rather
late in the day, but fearing his father might
want him on particular business, and anxious
promptly to obey his commands, he at once
took leave of his cousins and aunt: though in
the countenance of the latter, he perceived a certain malignant look, which would have explained to one more quick-sighted than himself,
that it arose from the satisfaction she experienced
in being so soon revenged.

Thus my father immediately departed: and passing through a village, he called on the Curate,
(who was an old friend of his father's,) to take

some refreshment. Having travelled some leagues, and having a still greater distance to go, the worthy Curate wished to persuade him to take a bed at his house, as the night was fast approaching; but the wish to obey the order of his parent, prevented his accepting this kind offer. His host, therefore, furnished him with a small bottle of wine, for his use on the road; and he and his servant departed. On reaching the end of the village, he began diverting himself by whistling and singing; his servant, who was a very young man, was much alarmed at this, and requested him not by any means to whistle or sing, for fear he should rouse the robbers, who might probably assassinate them; but giddy youth does not listen to reason: he laughed at his fears, and desired him not to be alarmed, as he had with him his faithful dog, who would not fail to give him notice of the approach of any person whatever, and a double-barrelled gun well loaded, and his hanger; but he could not quiet his servant's fears: so that when passing by a wood, whilst they were in a valley, my father whistled to his dog, and the echo reverberated the sound; it so terrified his servant, that he begged and prayed his master to take his gun from his shoulder and make ready, for he was certain he had heard the robbers whistle in the wood, which was answered by others, and that they would soon, no doubt, be attacked. My father told him that it was he himself who had whistled, and that it was the echo which he heard. He whistled, therefore, again, and the dog came to him without finding any thing; yet all was perfectly useless, for nothing could calm his fears. They, however, reached home in safety about midnight, and found the family, except a servant, all in bed. He retired, therefore, to rest, without seeing any other person that night. But though he himself did not rise very early the next morning, yet he found that his servant was not up, and on enquiry, he was informed that he was very ill; which my father, on visiting him, learnt to be really the case; and for a considerable time after, this man was actually confined to his bed, by the violence of a fever.

He now asked the servants if his father was apprised of his return, or had enquired after him; and was informed that he was gone to take his usual morning walk.

At the hour of dinner he returned; but before he reached the house, my father went out to meet him, to salute his hand according to custom; but he withdrew it from him, and cast such a look of displeasure upon him, as made him shudder. He wished, therefore, to know the cause; and asked, if he was dissatisfied with him, or if he had inadvertently committed any fault? he was, however, answered only by a glance of the eye, more severe than the first. He no longer doubted of his misfortune, that is to say, that his father had been prejudiced in his opinion against him, by some one, during his absence; but could not imagine from what source his parent's displeasure could arise: yet he entertained some hopes that before he went to bed, he might, perhaps, be able to extract the secret, which now appeared wrapt in such mystery; but it was in vain, for although he reiterated his request, neither his prayers, nor his tears, could disarm his father;

who retired to his apartment, without saying a word in explanation

With a heart full of sorrow, his son threw himself on his bed; and now, for the first time, Morpheus refused to close his eyes. All that he had done for months before, was made to pass in review before his mind; yet without his being able to discover any thing which could cause such unmerited anger in his parent: and thus he lost himself in vain conjecture. Two days had already elapsed, without terminating his sorrows; which now began to take such possession of his mind, as made him truly miserable and unhappy. The illness, also, of his servant became every day more dangerous, though nothing was neglected to promote his recovery, yet all failed in effect; his life consequently was pronounced by his medical attendants to be in danger; who also gave it as their opinion, that if he did survive, it would be a long time before he became convalescent.

This, therefore, induced my father to engage another servant; he also called upon an opulent Jew, of whom he solicited a loan of one hundred pounds, in ready money; which he obtained without much difficulty, as his father, since his return from the regiment, had made him his *Intendant;* and as he paid and received all accounts, and gave his receipts, &c. on all proper occasions.

He now collected every thing his father possessed of value, with the ready money he had in hand; and having thus arranged every thing, he questioned his new servant: asking him, if he was disposed to follow and share with

him his good or ill fortune, or whatever might
befall him? who at once replied, that he would
follow him wherever he chose to go, nor
would he leave him so long as he lived.
Having thus ascertained the feelings of his
servant, he then communicated his intended
project to him, and gave orders to have every
thing ready early the next morning, by break
of day, and to meet him with his two horses
at the garden gate; and that to prevent suspicion, he might tell the other servants he was
going to take a journey for a few days. Ah!
how long this tedious night appeared, which
he believed would, perhaps, be the last he
should ever pass under the paternal roof, and
of which he was going to take an eternal
adieu—a fatal farewell; which, however painful, he thought must be submitted to.

As soon as Aurora appeared, he arose,
dressed himself hastily, and sought his father's
apartment; who, astonished to see him, eagerly
enquired the cause of his coming to disturb
him at so early an hour? At these words, his
son could not restrain himself any longer; his
tears flowed in abundance, and his agonized
feelings, for the moment, deprived him of
utterance. He now perceived his father was
much affected by this scene; as soon, therefore, as he could articulate his words, he fell
on his knees by the bed side, and seizing one
of his father's hands, in spite of a feeble resistance, he saluted it, and said, "Hear, for
the *last* time, your unhappy son!"—Words
which he could scarely pronounce, before a
fresh torrent of tears stifled his speech;—at
length, becoming rather more calm, he thus

continued : "Since my arrival from Ph...., in vain have I done every thing I could devise, to find out what crime I could possibly have committed, but without being able to learn one word from you in explanation on this subject : know then, Sir, I can no longer support your displeasure ; and since I have lost (without knowing the cause,) your friendship and confidence, it will be impossible for me to live under the same roof with you ; for each day would inflict a more severe blow to my aching heart : I therefore, now come to crave one more favour from you, and which I pray you will not refuse,—your last blessing ; after which, I am going to embark at St..... for America ;—all is ready, I have the sum of one hundred pounds, which I borrowed of F...., here are my accompts, you will see my receipts and disbursements, and I dare hope you will honour the bill of exchange I have given to F...., as here is a deed wherein I surrender all right and title to whatever might hereafter devolve to me ; for I shall not, most assuredly, ever set foot again where I have been so unfortunate, as without knowing why or wherefore, to incur your highest displeasure. If, on the contrary, my voyage should be propitious, and that by my good fortune, I should be able to contribute to the happiness of a father, who will be ever dear to me, in spite of his injustice."—At these words, his father could no longer restrain his parental feelings ; and said, " No, my son, you shall not fly from a father, whose miseries would only be increased by your absence : your tears are to me a sure guarantee that I shall yet be able to instil into your mind, those sacred principles suitable to your birth, and what I consider due to the memory of your ancestors. I have been informed, you secretly pay your addresses to Caroline, your cousin's female servant; for this reason I recalled you home, and if I have since that time appeared severe, it is only from the grief of my heart, for having given birth to a son, who could wish so to dishonour me and himself. O that I had but been informed of this circumstance in time; alas! it is now too late: if it be true that your affection is fixed on this girl, it will be plunging a dagger into the heart of your unfortunate father; who, if he has committed a fault, it is in having loved you too well." From this recital, my father instantly knew that his parent's displeasure originated in the malice of his aunt; and said, "This blow is inflicted by a hand which was formely dear to me, but which, from this moment, I hold in abhorrence: in a word, it is from your sister, for I will not again call that woman—aunt, who could wish to disunite the father's affections from his son, and the husband's from the wife; on the latter subject I shall draw a veil, for it will be too painful to delineate what she is capable of doing, when impelled by revenge." Being a little more calm, he said, "If this is all, be perfectly satisfied, in a few hours I will convince you of my innocence. I shall not relate to you the circumstances myself, but the hand which penned those fatal lines, which have occasioned your torment and my own, shall be compelled to write my justification."— His father, already convinced, clasped his son to his breast, saying, "Oh! my son, if what you have said is true, which I cannot doubt, I shall then be happy; had it been as I feared, you would in a short time have followed me to my grave." Disengaging himself from this tender paternal embrace, so dear to him, he hastened, not on the road to America, but on that of Ph...., where he soon arrived. Dismounting, he ordered his faithful servant to have the horses well refreshed and attended to, and himself instantly sought his cousins, who were already down stairs, but not so his wicked aunt; he related to them the whole particulars, without exaggeration: they could scarcely restrain their astonishment and indignation, or conceive how it could be possible, to be so deliberately wicked, as to carry revenge to such lengths. "Be satisfied, cousin," said all of them, "that in defending your cause, we shall justify our Caroline's, whose reputation has been attacked more even than your own, and we all know she is very discreet." The aunt was instantly requested to come down stairs; my father, meanwhile, was hid in a closet, by their desire; and on her appearance in the saloon, his three cousins only were seen, one of whom was married, and the other two were above being trifled with, and would warmly resent the least imputation, particularly from other females; they never failed, therefore, in well defending their own causes on all occasions.

On the aunt's appearance, she was soon literally overwhelmed with their volubility, and most pertinent questions; to whom her evasive and equivocating answers, made her appear still more guilty. At length, finally to disconcert her, the signal was given for my

father's appearance, who instantly came forward; her whole face now became a deep
crimson, but it was not the coloring of timidity
or bashfulness, but of anger, rage, and shame
combined; and she did not fail to load him
with every kind of abusive epithets she could
make use of, or malice invent, but this did
not prevent her being obliged herself to write
that her former letter was calumnious; though
in part to spare her honour, she was allowed to
add, that it was written in a moment of anger,
which had been occasioned by her nephew's
refusing to accompany her to the vintage.
My father was also furnished with a letter,
written in the name of, and signed by all three
of his cousins; stating that his conduct whilst
with them, had been perfectly correct, and
void of all reproach. And on obtaining these
precious documents, which surpassed his most
sanguine expectations, he mounted his horse;
nor will any one doubt his making the best
of his way homeward, though it were at the
risk of killing those valuable animals, by the
continued speed at which they were kept the
whole of the way. On his return home, he
again threw himself at his father's feet, presenting both letters. The one from his cousins
was first opened; and when his father had
finished its perusal, he raised his son, calling
him by the most endearing names; and what
was infinitely more important, promised him
for the future, never to be prejudiced by any
one against him; and that should any thing
hereafter be attempted to be insinuated against
him, he would immediately acquaint him with
the circumstances. For sometime my ancestor
would not even condescend to open his sister's

letter ; but when, after many entreaties, he was induced to comply, what was his astonishment and indignation, when he read that she herself contradicted her former calumny ? He exclaimed, "My son, this circumstance will increase my affection for you, and if it be possible, it will equal the contempt in which I shall henceforth hold my sister ; and I now clearly perceive how much I have been the dupe, and deceived by her : but it shall be so no more; all is now over between us ; she shall no longer remain under my roof, where she had still resided, even after the death of your grandmother."

After this mutual explanation, my father possessed more than ever, the whole confidence of his parent, sharing with him his moments of grief and happiness. He described to his son, the opulence which our family formerly enjoyed ; at the same time, explaining the reasons of the decay into which it had fallen. My father then said, if he would give him permission, he would go to America, he having previously had some conversation on this subject, with a person in the neighbourhood, who had been established there, and had, in a comparatively short time, realized an ample fortune ; and who had represented to him, that if he was successful in his enterprize, he might perhaps be enabled to reinstate the family in its ancient lustre. His father was much pleased at the idea thus suggested ; but unwilling wholly to trust to speculation, never would consent to his son's going there alone, but said, he would speak to this person himself : and farther, if what had been advanced, was fully

E

proved to his satisfaction, and the project appeared feasible, he would decide in the affirmative, and would go with his son himself; and that he would then dispose of part of his property, for its value in specie; and that they would take with them a limited number of men and women of the neighbourhood, in indigent circumstances, (if inclined to go with them,) and establish a colony in the new world:—and that if it should once become flourishing, they should return home for the remainder of the family.—His mother, sister, and brother, should remain in Europe, until this new colony was well established.

Proper arrangements were made, for the interview with this opulent person, who had returned from America;—but very little interesting information could be obtained from him: for this reason, the most authentic writings on this subject were procured; but my ancestor never could be fully convinced of the practicability of the scheme; being ever unwilling to trust his property on uncertain speculations: and therefore, after much trouble and diligent investigation, the project was ultimately abandoned.

Soon after, my father was ordered to replace one of his fellow officers, in a detachment at Est....., who, from personal quarrels, &c. had been on bad terms with the inhabitants there; in consequence of which, he was obliged to solicit his recall:—the cause originated in the following circumstances.—The village of Est....., is about the worst and meanest village in the country; his quarters were at a paltry alehouse, which had only two apartments below stairs; one of which was used as a kitchen, and even bed-chamber, by the mistress of the house; the other was occupied by this officer. At the feast, the people not having room enough in the kitchen, took, without ceremony, and in his absence, possession of the officer's apartment; who, on his return, (in about an hour,) found his room completely filled by these unwelcome gentry: of this he highly disapproved; whilst one of them, on his entrance, came forward and made his awkward excuses, in the name of the company; at the same time, offering him to drink with them, presenting a large goblet, which held nearly a pint, and from which they all drank in their turn, according to their usual custom;—he somewhat bluntly refused their request, for which reason they ill treated him on every occasion that presented itself; which ultimately obliged him to solicit his recall, and my father received orders to replace him.

On his arrival, he assembled the whole detachment, which was dispersed in four different villages, and thus addressed them:—"Soldiers, you know well what has occurred to my predecessor, who has left you; on which consideration, I prohibit all of you, under pain of being dismissed from the detachment, from ever drinking with any of those men; I shall take proper care to have your provisions regularly supplied, which duty I shall personally attend to." After this admonition, he dismissed them, distributing some money amongst them for their present refreshment;—they all promised to obey his injunction on every occasion; and at once shouted, "Long live our Lieutenant! with him we shall not fail to be happy; he is a father to his soldiers."

After having taken a proper survey of the place, my father ordered patroles at different hours, though a fortnight elapsed without the least disturbance;—and during the time he remained there, no differences occurred in the village or neighbourhood.

His merit, accordingly, did not escape the notice of his Prince, and he was regularly promoted; which occasioned some jealousy among the officers in command with him, who endeavoured to disconcert all his plans, in secret; in which, sometimes, they were but too successful. This unjust conduct could scarcely be brooked, by a mind sanguine and impetuous like my father's, whose bosom glowed with military ardour and enthusiasm; but he generally found means to defeat their utmost efforts, and continued in favour with his Prince, who was constantly giving him fresh proofs f his high approbation and kindness, which had the effect of still more increasing the animosity of his enemies; who had recourse to every species of calumny and detraction, to create doubts even of the motives of his actions, the most generous and disinterested of which, were, by insinuations and misrepresentations, weakened as much as possible in their effect, and sometimes represented as flowing from a diametrically opposite motive.

It required no small degree of discrimination, care, and attention, to counteract the effect of

such unmerited conduct: more than once has
my father been prevented, by his then superior
officers, from having recourse to his sword, to
silence calumniators; but not being able to
obtain satisfaction in the honourable way he
wished, he redoubled his vigilance in performing every duty incumbent on him as an officer
and gentleman;—in alleviating the wants,
endeavouring to increase the comforts, and
promoting discipline in the men under his
command: who all looked up to him with
confidence, when their grievances called for
redress; nor was he ever appealed to in vain.

He was progressively raised in rank and
favour by his Prince, until he was promoted to
Lieut. Col. *Commandant* of a regiment of
rangers, bearing his own name. He had been
frequently heard to say, that the sacred principles of religion, virtue, and honour, instilled
into his mind by his worthy ecclesiastical preceptor, and grandmother, were never obliterated or effaced from his memory, through the
whole course of his earthly career;—but afforded him consolation and comfort in the
most trying scenes of adversity and persecution; a larger share of which, has fallen to the
lot of few individuals, of which, the full particulars will be detailed in their due order
in the course of this narrative.

I will now furnish my readers with some
account of my mother, her family, &c. but as
on this topic, very little information can be
gathered from any documents in my possession,
a circumstance I certainly regret,—I shall
principally relate those particulars which are
well known to me.

My mother was the eldest daughter of the Sieur Noel Després de Wallers, near Chimay; who was considered the richest and most respectable person of the district in which he resided :——benevolent and charitable to all around him, he was universally and justly esteemed by all who knew him;. from merit, more than the influence of wealth. He married Miss Desprèz, his relation, who was equally rich, viz. the family of Maschelazt, (on the mother's side,) having a title of nobility, which her ample fortune enabled her to support in its ancient dignity and splendour; keeping a very large establishment, and holding a very distinguished rank in the country. She had the misfortune to lose her mother in her infancy. She was much beloved by her grandfather, who had a sister, a Mother Abbess, in a convent in the order of *Poor Clares*, in the vicinity of Douai, where my mother was placed at an early age, for instruction, and to have inculcated and promoted into her juvenile mind, those sacred principles of religion and moral duty, from which she never deviated. To this source she always attributed her solace and comfort, in her severe afflictions.

She was extremely indulged, and often permitted, although very young, to join her relations and friends in parties of amusement at Treïlon, the residence of her aunt, and at the country seat at Lasnoi de Brochè, and Flayon.

At Anor, my grandfather had an extensive iron foundery and glass manufactory; as, likewise, another in the forest du Pont de Seine, part of which forest belonged to him. These extensive manufactories were principally carried on under the direction of approved workmen, in each particular branch; and were very lucrative.

My mother was naturally humane and very benevolent to the poor; for this purpose, she had some considerable sums placed at her own disposal, for charitable purposes only;—which she applied so successfully in relieving the present wants of the indigent poor, that nothing could exceed the gratitude of her needy dependents, whom she regularly visited; and, consequently, she had the happiness to see the fruits of her benevolence producing comfort, comparative ease, and cheerfulness, in them all :—who, as it were, though indigent, forgot their anxious cares and hard destiny in her presence, and loaded her with their benedictions; which to a feeling mind like hers, was an ample reward for all her exertions in their behalf, to promote their future welfare.

At the death of my grandfather, my mother's sister, Nettalie, was left under the immediate care of my mother; but who, from an accidental fall from her horse, when riding out on an excursion of pleasure, received such a violent contusion on the head, that although she escaped the accident with life, yet never, after this period, completely recovered her mental faculties; she was, for this reason, placed in a convent for protection, not as a sister nun, but to live in their society and retirement;—having the liberty of egress and regress at all seasonable times, and being always accompanied by an attendant from the convent.

My mother's uncle was the officiating clergyman at Chimay; but who, through the Revolution, lost his whole personal property; and, from severe persecution, was obliged to conceal himself for upwards of six months, in his house; a faithful servant bringing him, at stated times, as opportunities offered, provisions for his sustenance: but who could never be prevailed on to divulge the place of his revered master's incarceration, which had frequently, although ineffectually, been attempted to be discovered by his implacable enemies.

Monsieur, the general Desprèz le Polonois, cousin to my mother, is now resident at Anor.

At the age of seventeen, my mother was married to Monsieur Dumez de Rilly, who was of the most respectable family and connections in the neighbourhood of Avesnes; and an officer in the army: by whom she had two sons, the eldest Louis Michæl Dumez de Rilly, the younger Louis Dumez: unfortunately, however, he suddenly burst a blood vessel, at the very time that he had a large party of friends, to spend the evening with him at his own house. Anxious, therefore, to conceal as long as possible, this fatal injury, he was at length compelled, from extreme weakness and loss of blood, to retire; requesting, moreover, his servant not to disturb the harmony and conviviality of his guests, by mentioning to any of them his perilous situation. Surgical assistance was immediately procured; but in vain; every effort made by the medical attendants, failed of success: and nothing could exceed the consternation and dismay of the party, when informed he was no more, and that he had expired in the night.

My mother was inconsolable for the loss of so affectionate an husband, whose life had passed in the interesting energies of a useful and honourable activity; the animated emanations of a sound and enlightened understanding, which made the deep thrillings of generous affection and tender sympathy, the sweet reciprocations of confidence and esteem, the enraptured perceptions of intellectual good, the modest but joyful sense of conscious worth, the towerings of a noble ambition, those highest satisfactions, which give the chief relish, and dignity to life, all, all had fled, with this tender partner of her life, so suddenly snatched away for ever! who but a few short hours before had been in the enjoyment of health, and happy amidst his friends; in the possession of every worldly blessing; little thinking in how short a time he would be called into futurity!

What an awful lesson to his gay companions, and indeed to every one; to be always prepared for this great change, for we know not when we may be called hence. The uncertainty of all sublunary things, and the certainty of death, which spares neither youth or age, or sex; the consideration that we are not certain of even the fleeting moment, must surely convince us of the infinite danger of delay; yet human nature is so apt to procrastinate, fondly hoping that the short span of life may be prolonged, until perhaps as suddenly called into eternity, as the example now before us; leaving but a very short time indeed for concerns of the most infinitely vast importance,—the salvation of our souls.

This is the second instance recorded in this narrative of sudden death, from accidental causes, which 1 trust will plead a sufficient apology to the reader for this degression, (if apology be deemed necessary) who may rest assured it arises from the purest motive of doing good ; and that it may have this effect is my most earnest wish.

After the funeral obsequies and months of sorrow and mourning, my mother turned her attention principally to the instruction of her children. When the mind is harrassed by misfortune and sorrow, the judgment is too apt to be in some measure biassed, notwithstanding a sincere wish to the contrary. My mother accordingly seemed to find her children the chief solace to her grief, and therefore a very long time elapsed before she could be prevailed on to join in the friendly parties of her relations ; though after their continued and repeated solicitations, she was induced at length to comply with their wishes, at intervals, which afforded sometimes a temporary relief to her agonized mind.

If men are commonly, and as I presume for the most part, justly supposed to possess greater strength of mind, in science, in council, in action, and in danger ; let them acknowledge, however, that in generosity of soul, and nobleness of attachment, they are sometimes at least equalled by women : instances are familiar to me, of females having displayed on many occasions, a courage truly heroic, sacrificing every comfort to relieve the miseries of a relation, or a friend in distress; surmounting every obstacle and danger, to accomplish this desired object; and not unfrequently have been known to succeed, beyond their most sanguine expectations.——What a rich reward for their generous, and noble exertions in behalf of the unfortunate!

But to return to my narrative, at length my mother was induced by her friends to join in their different parties, and once more to move as before in the circle of their friendly intercourse; which by degrees gradually dissipated the gloom on her mind, much to the satisfaction of her friends, and more particularly to her more near and dear relations: she thus found her serenitude of mind gradually restored, when occasionally mixing in select society. Social intercourse therefore, with its enlivening charms reconciled her by its influence, and time, tempered with the lenient powers of religion, composed a balm to heal her wounded spirits.

At this period, a series of ignoble petty tyrants were permitted to outrage every feeling of humanity, in my unhappy country; by the plunder and spoliation of the opulent, and subversion of all established order.——It was sufficient at this time to be of noble birth, to be marked out for a victim of persecution, and not unfrequently of destruction.——Unhappy France doomed to send forth the flower of her youth to the tented field crimsoned with human gore, trembled to her basis, but durst scarcely ejaculate her groans; espionage, imprisonment, and death, were the order of the day, during this reign of terror: though some persons made

most rapid fortunes, by taking advantage of
the general devastation. Even the sabbath
was profaned by every irregularity; it was no
more regarded than any other day of the week,
nor did it occasion any interruption of public
business. He who most notoriously trans-
gressed the divine laws, in this particular,
thought himself superior to the rest of mankind.—What glory can possibly result from
sporting with that worship, which a weak mortal owes to the Supreme Being? The sabbaths
were turned into decades; and while religion
was so grossly neglected, and the people accustomed to see the religion of their ancestors
daily reviled, they learned to think of it with the
greatest indifference; and soon became ripe
for the ridiculous celebrations of the festival
of the Goddess of Reason, &c.—What destination awaited men distinguished for purity of
manners, and decided friends to the welfare
of their country, may, from hence, be easily
deduced by every one. Indeed, a most melancholy sensation is produced, by merely con-
templating the immense number of gentlemens'
seats in ruins, formerly the property of persons
who were then obliged to forsake their country,
or who had become the victims of the *guillotine*.
And this sensation is still augmented, in beholding what once probably was the abode of
munificence and hospitality, now, perhaps,
only occupied by a peasant, or by a labourer and
his family,—the dilapidated mansion,—the
abode of squalid misery and want,—wretched-
ness and misery,—the portion of its possessor.
From this slight sketch may be seen, the sad
effects of lawless power, and subversion of
order in the government: this same country,

but a few short years previously to these events, under the sway of the most amiable of monarchs, now a prey to anarchy and tyranny, the enemy and scourge of the neighbouring kingdoms, nay, I might say, almost of all Europe : committing every enormity, under the specious names of liberty and equality, by order of their self-elected petty tyrants of the day.

At this period my father was with his regiment, at Avesnes, visiting in the first circles of the place, and frequently meeting my mother in different parties. He was much respected as an officer, and as a gentleman, by the inhabitants; ever keeping the strictest discipline and due subordination in his men :—although lenient and indulgent to them on proper occasions, yet he never overlooked any deviation from their duty ; the slightest breach of which, would be sure to receive his marked displeasure. On the other hand, he invariably obtained a redress of their grievances, when represented to him ; and was always esteemed as the soldiers' friend and benefactor. This impartial conduct was approved and commended by all who knew him: so different from the despotic conduct of some of his predecessors, whose principal motive of action seemed to be, to tyrannise over all who were unfortunately under their command;—quite an opposite mode of conduct was invariably followed by my father; strict discipline maintained, yet always ready to conciliate every difference between parties, and ever to avoid arbitary or despotic decisions ; let them emanate from whom they might; they were sure to

meet with his strongest opposition and ulti‑
mate rejection.

My father, at this place visiting in the same
parties with my mother, an intimate acquaint‑
ance was insensibly formed between them;
which, by degrees, ripened into the most
disinterested friendship,—that noble relation,
so superior to the common connections of
birth or accident,—that delightful union of the
mind, which is formed by intimacy, founded on
esteem,—sanctified by virtue, cememented by
a similarity of views and inclinations, and
preserved by the reciprocation of kindness and
confidence,—of sympathy and zeal:—the
comfort and dignity attendant on an animated
but calm reciprocation of esteem and com‑
plaisance,—the enchanting ties by which
hearts are often united, with an appropriation
ineffably endearing, from the numberless pur‑
poses of private delight and felicity.

I am convinced that honourable love is the
will and the work of the common parent of us
all; and we know that the state of life to
which it naturally tends, was appointed by
him from the beginning of ages:—it is the
bond and cement of society, the wishes of the
heart pointed from the best of principles to a
worthy object, which deserves to be happy in
its possession, on account of its purity and
elevation. It has been long agreed, that as
soon as this ennobling energy is mutually
experienced, the usual ideas of splendour and
affluence, rank and fashion, will fade from the
imagination; and often that retirement will be
accompanied with a satisfaction, which the

bustle of company and the parade of fortune can never confer.

Formed to increase the comforts and diminish the sorrows of life, by a tender and unwearied participation of both, and placed in situations most friendly to the polishing the mind and manners; my mother reaped from a virtuous education, all those advantages which become inestimable in their future conduct in life. And when the heart becomes more fixed by an appropriating passion for one individual, the enlivening and refining energy is then most happily experienced. My father, naturally of an ardent mind, his benevolent affections assumed a vigour and sweetness unobserved before; he seemed to rise above himself: his friendly disposition, ambitious of preserving her approbation, attended with an assimilating influence on his character, indulged in a generous glow of amity and conscious greatness, unspeakably soothing to the soul; that seldom appears so amiable or respectable, as when expanding in kindred minds, and pursuing plans of communicating happiness in all the social affections, mixed with a certain complacency and strong desire to please, joined to a circumspect behaviour, which rendered him more particularly dear to all his friends and acquaintance; possessing great assiduity, discretion, and perseverance, added to true politeness, with lively and agreeable sentiments, and a manner of expressing them, at once natural and delicate. Who knows not, that we slide insensibly, yet rapidly, into a resemblance of those we so much admire?

Between two minds tuned to one another, there may be much diversity in many particular notes, but the general ground and air are the same; and the different parts combined, serve only to complete the unison and harmony of the whole. This delightful friendly intercourse was, by time, ripened into affection and mutual love; and with the approbation of all parties on either side concerned, they were united in the holy bond of wedlock, on the twenty third day of October, 1792, at Le Quesnoy; but most certainly at an impropitious period; that is to say, during the French Revolution:—of the horrors of which, no one can form an adequate idea, or of its dreadful effects, much as has been heard on this subject, unless they had been at the time in this devoted country. We shall have frequent occasion to refer to this period in the sequel; I shall, therefore, proceed with my narrative. During the residence of my mother and her two sons in La Quesnoy, the place was besieged, and closely blockaded; all egress and regress completely cut off: to retreat was impossible; they were, therefore, obliged to remain, and witness all the horrors of the siege. There being no alternative left, they were compelled to submit, and make a virtue of necessity as far as was practicable.

At this awful period, the author of these Memoirs drew her first breath, on the twenty eighth day of May, 1793; amidst the thunder of artillery, the incessant roar of volleys of musketry, and frequent discharges of bombs, throw into the town by the besiegers. A shell penetrated the apartment where my

mother and her helpless infant then lay, broke
a cauldron, at the time on the fire, into atoms,
and dispersed into pieces in every direction
about the chamber; which spread terror and
dismay amongst all the domestic attendants
then present, who immediately fled for the
safety and preservation of their lives, to the
cellars below ground, leaving my poor mother,
then in an extremely weak state, and myself her
infant, to all the horrors and imminent dangers
of this appalling scene: but who, though
almost exausted from weakness, fatigue, and
alarm, placed her whole trust and confidence in
Him alone, whose invisible hand only could
shield us from impending destruction. Her
secret prayers to the Almighty were not made
in vain: we were preserved,—I must say
miraculously preserved uninjured!—Amidst so
many impending dangers, we remained not
only safe, but unhurt; to the utter astonishment of all those who had deserted us at
this awful crisis of imminent danger, and who
had, no doubt, anticipated a very different result;
scarcely believing it possible we could escape,
and who fully expected we had both perished:—
but what must have been their astonishment
and gratitude to that Omnipotent Being,
whose arm had shielded us from the threat-
ening dangers, to find us still in existence and
wholly uninjured?—for although my mother was
nearly exhausted from extreme weakness and
alarm, which from natural causes might have
been anticipated, especially in so perilous a
situation; still the escape was deemed by every
one most providential.

From the strictness of the blockade and

F

great scarcity of provisions in the garrison, inconceivable deprivations and hardships were experienced; at length, the most common necessaries of life could scarcely be procured, even at the most exhorbitant prices; and although every expedient was tried, no fresh supplies of provisions could be thrown into the town to relieve the garrison. The pressure of want became at last so great, that the inhabitants were obliged, with the garrison, to supply their wants with such food as at other times they would have rejected with disdain; but there was no alternative, the cravings of hunger must be in some way appeased, to preserve existence. When these pangs had in some measure been relieved by the scanty supply, they were satiated only for the moment, and would therefore return again with redoubled violence, before any thing farther could be procured, with the miserable expectation of a still increasing scarcity, and the dreadful anticipation, that shortly this very scanty supply which was daily diminishing, would soon totally cease. I shall dwell no longer on these appalling scenes of my infancy; suffice it to say, the place was at length compelled to capitulate, and the blockade was of course removed; the distresses of the inhabitants were immediately relieved, or as greatly alleviated, as circumstances would allow, by the humanity of the besiegers; who, when they had taken possession of the place, treated the inhabitants with lenity, and even kindness; dissipating their alarm, and affording as prompt assistance as was possible, to all who most needed it, by distributing fresh provisions and every kind of relief which before had been so long denied them, and wholly prevented; to the inexpressible joy of the poor sufferers, who had not anticipated such a favorable result when oppressed with hunger, and the melancholy dread of still greater privations, which all vanished on the surrender of the place.

My mother, compelled by untoward events passing in such rapid succession, to consult the personal safety of herself and children, retired to Avesnes. When we had reached Mons, we were all thrown into prison, and there confined for the space of three weeks; but on being released, we proceeded on this painful journey, labouring under every kind of calamity.—Our misfortunes still increasing, we were arrested a second time, and experienced the severest treatment merely on account of our title, which at this period was a sanction for inflicting the most unjust, the most flagrant outrages the mind can conceive, without the slightest personal provocation.—We were, however, again released after a time, and persevered on our miserable journey: but on our arrival at Avesnes, new sources of misery seemed to await our destined family:—our whole property was seized, and ordered to be confiscated, and ourselves to be thrown into prison; from which confinement we could not for a considerable time get released: nor from the unmerited sufferings and wanton cruelty heaped upon our devoted heads. At length, after the repeated intercessions of my father, we were once more liberated; but only to experience accumulating distress and misery; being afterwards deprived of all our property, for the recovery of which many fruitless attempts were made by my parents. Yet ineffectual as these applications had hitherto proved, a glimmering of hope still remained, to cheer our despondency a little; and by constant and unwearied perseverance in these applications, incessantly renewed, we at length succeeded in obtaining the restoration of a small portion of the family property, situate at Wallers, the residence of my grandfather; likewise that at Floretine, at Ouvenel Glazon, at Treilon, and at Anor; but very small indeed was the portion thus restored to us at each place; taking into consideration the amount and value of the property confiscated, and that nearly three years had elapsed before the restitution of even this small part of the family estates was acceded to; and that, even when granted, much difficulty and trouble was experienced at each particular place where the restitution was ordered, and that obstacles of every kind were fabricated; various subterfuges and evasions, nay, every trick that could be devised resorted to, in order to delay, and if possible, to prevent the ultimate restitution. In this precarious state of uncertainty and comparative indigence, was our family kept, by the petty chicanery and wrangling of the local possessors of the property, for several years; and never could obtain the whole even of this inconsiderable part of their former possessions.

In a ramble to a village called Ouvenelles, about half a league distant, my mother discovered, near a water mill, some elder blossoms overhanging the water; at this time wanting some for medicinal purposes, she stepped on a large branch of the tree, to be able to reach them. After gathering a few bunches, the branch suddenly broke off, and my parent was immediately precipitated head long into the stream below; my cries of alarm soon reached the miller and his family, who instantly ran to the spot, and very fortunately were in sufficient time to rescue my poor mother from drowning; and who very humanely placed her in one of their beds in the cottage, kindly affording every relief in their power, to endeavour to restore suspended animation, which after much difficulty, and many repeated efforts from these good peasants, was at length attended with the desired success: several days, however, elapsed before it was deemed safe to remove her to her own house; and for a considerable time afterwards, my mother required the care of her medical attendants at home.—From the violence and suddenness of the shock on her nervous system, febrile symptoms were produced; and several weeks passed before she was again rendered, through the skill of these medical gentlemen, convalescent.

Thus once more restored to health, the miserable situation of our pecuniary affairs, at this period, preyed on her mind. Still weak, and subject to frequent nervous irritability, which, though she had never before experienced any symtoms of the kind, produced such depression and lowness of spirits, (added to the cause above related,) as soon made a rapid inroad on her constitution, which was gradually becoming more enfeebled by these combined anxieties and miseries; which not only required a much stronger constitution to bear them, (without experiencing these fatal injuries and shocks so frequently repeated,) but in fact, a vigour of mind and body that could avert their ill effects; but these unfortunately she did not possess at this melancholy period, nor could it indeed be expected, all circumstances duly considered.

My father, with a consummate knowledge of mankind, a robust constitution, sanguine disposition, acknowledged perseverance, and a fund of useful information, acquired by his professional intercourse with the higher classes of society, had the utmost difficulty with life, to weather the revolutionary storms, and the loss of his property which was inevitable; no exertions even strained to the highest pitch, could avert the evil: such was the rapacity and tyranny of those miscreants at the head of affairs, that the utmost efforts of human power were ineffectual to its preservation.

The instability of human grandeur was at this period most conspicuous:—an awful death-like gloom prevailed every where; as the revolutionary committee imprisoned greater part of the most respectable inhabitants, many of whom were dispatched to the capital, to be mocked by a pretended examination, and sentenced by that most diabolical institution—the revolutionary tribunal, with the mere outward form of a trial; frequently on charges of the most trivial nature, totally void of foundation, or even probability; for the very purpose of confiscating their property and possessions.

No one can form an adequate idea of the great enormities committed in the names of Reason and Liberty, or of the horrors perpetrated by these self-elected petty tyrants, who were the scourge and dread of every respectable person within their influence; nothing could scarcely escape their rapacity, nor was any thing too monstrous for them to hesitate about its execution. Among the various diversified occurrences which at different periods have occupied the attention of mankind, and employed the pen of the historian, none have appeared in modern times more important in itself, or more likely to excite the interest of posterity, than this tremendous moral convulsion — the French Revolution. The wonderful effects it had produced in Europe, are generally known: very few indeed, of the continental kingdoms escaped its rapacity; in fact, for a time the gigantic strides of these despots seemed to threaten them with total subversion; which, if even secured by the loss of their best blood and treasure, for a respite from their encroachments, were constantly liable to fresh aggressions, as caprice or policy dictated.

In the winter of 1794, the French armies marched into Holland; a few days after their arrival, the French commissioners with the army published a proclamation, in which they told the Dutch " In the midst of war we consider you as our friends and allies; it is under this name that we enter your country; we seek not to terrify, but to inspire you with confidence. It is but a few years since a tyrannic conqueror prescribed to you laws; we abolish them and restore to you your freedom: we come not to make you slaves;——the French nation shall preserve to you your independence;——personal safety shall be secured, and property protected."

Seven days after this proclamation, the same commissioners, having been admitted with their troops into all the towns, &c. published a second proclamation, in which they formally directed the Dutch government to furnish the army, within one month, with the following supplies, viz. 200,000 quintals of wheat, 500,000 rations of hay, 200,000 rations of straw, 500,000 bushels of corn, 150,000 pairs of shoes, 20,000 pairs of boots, 20,000 coats and waist-coats, 150,000 pairs of pantaloons, 200,000 shirts, and 50,000 hats; and besides all this, 12,000 oxen, to be delivered in two months. This requisition they called their amicable intentions, &c. and gave the Dutch to understand, that in case the articles were not furnished, they should be exacted by force.

This, however, was only the commencement; — they kept their armies in Holland during the winter, took every thing they wanted, and paid in depreciated Assignats at par; and finally forced the Dutch to form an offensive and defensive alliance with them against England for ever. This treaty was signed May 15, 1795. It obliged the Dutch to cede to France, " as indemnities," two of their most important frontier towns, with the adjoining territories, and one of their provinces, to admit French garrisons, in case of war in that quarter, into three of their strongest frontier towns, one of their principal sea-ports, &c.; to employ half their forces in carrying on the recent campaign, under French generals; and finally, to pay France, as a farther indemnification for the expences of the war, one hundred million of livres; equal to twenty five millions of dollars, in cash or bills of exchange on foreign countries, &c. &c. In return, the French drove away the Stadtholder, and changed the government; but did not suffer the Dutch to adopt one to their own mind. The Dutch brought upon themselves, in addition to all these proofs of amity, an offensive and defensive war against England, in which they lost all their rich possessions in the East Indies, &c. a great part of their fleet, and the remains of their trade.

In an enumeration of French requisitions, the losses of the Dutch are estimated at the enormous sum of thirty four millions sterling.

The French armies entered Belgium under repeated and solemn promises of protection and freedom. No sooner had they obtained possession of this unfortunate country, than they put every article of property which could be of use to them, into requisition, and compelled the people to receive payment in depreciated Assignats at par; levied immense contributions; ordered measures to be taken to compel the people to exchange their money for Assignats at par; placed the country under the government of military commissioners, &c. and having thus afforded "liberty and protection" to the Belgians, having thus "broken their chains," &c. they proceeded to confiscate for their own use, the whole property of the clergy in Belgium, to the amount of more than two hundred and fifty millions of dollars.——This is a faint sketch of a few of the aggressions of the French Republican governors. I shall not however, in this place cite any other instance on the subject, but resume my narrative·

My father at this period employed most of his leisure hours in chemical researches, making experiments on an extensive scale ; in which large sums were expended. He ultimately acquired a sufficient knowledge of this useful art, to benefit society by some important discoveries ; which with his usual disinterestedness were immediately communicated to the public, without ever requiring the smallest remuneration for his assiduous labours. Although the chimerical idea of commuting metals into gold, or searching for the philosopher's stone, was with some a prevalent idea, yet my father never for a moment entertained such visionary prospects : all his researches tended to benefit science by his new discoveries ; leaving to others, by their promulgation, the means of reaping the benefit, which was only due to the party who at considerable expence and labour had first made the discovery.

My father one day sauntering in the superb rooms at A....., appropriated to gaming, without any intention of partaking in the fascinating amusement, was, however, soon induced to join a party at *rouge et noir ;* at first he was tolerably successful ; but after alternate changes, the fickle goddess, fortune, forsook him, and he found himself completely drained of all his cash, (which was no inconsiderable sum :) thus he determined if possible to retrieve some part of his lost property ; and for this purpose, a valuable gold repeater which he had with him, being produced, it procured for him a temporary supply of cash, but which like the former was soon ingulphed in the same vortex of dissipation. Retiring without a shilling, and his mind harrassed with the most poignant feelings of regret, he left the place with the firm resolution never to enter it more. This afforded him a salutary lesson to avoid for the future the fatal rock on which so many others had split; and he wholly renounced for ever after, this dangerous amusement.

The Battalion de Poly, under my father's command, was soon after disbanded by order of the republican general Dampierre, and the Baron de Poly declared to have acted contrary to the then existing laws; in retaining to the said battalion his own name. The men were drafted into different regiments, but they had been so well disciplined, and taught by their revered commander to venerate their Sovereign, that they never could be induced to take any oath derogatory to the Bourbons. Their *Commandant* was proscribed in November, 1793, for his persevering loyalty to his Sovereign and country; his person seized, his papers sealed up, by order of John Francis Jourdain, at Troyes; but nothing found to criminate their victim at this time.

No sooner was the Baron de Poly liberated, than with determined perseverance in the cause of his illustrious master, in concert with Le Clerc Marquis de Vrainville, and other adherents of his Majesty, he was strenuously exerting every possible means in his power, to re-establish the lawful authority; and by this means restore to his distracted country, her former tranquillity and felicity. To accomplish this desirable object, he could

never desist; it was the wish of his heart, and
the mainspring of all his efforts. He joined
the agency which his most Christian Majesty
had in Paris, with Monsieur Bedouet, general
inspector of the Chañon Posts, &c. in communi-
nication with the loyal army in La Vendeé;
whose movements were arranged and directed
by them, as the necessity of the occasion required. For his eminent services at this period, he was offered the Cross of St. Louis,
which, with his usual disinterestedness he declined accepting; Brotier, Duverne, de Prailes,
Berthelot, de la Villeurney, M. de Bonnaire
Chevalier of the order of Malta, Ramel,
Malo, &c. at this period acted in concert with
them. To facilitate his communication with
the Marquis de Vrainville, their residences
were chosen contiguous to each other at Paris;
where private meetings were held of the different partizans of the king, and the best means
in their power divised, for ultimately obtaining
the object so anxiously and earnestly desired.
But what must have been my father's great surprise and indignation at this eventful period,
when their plans and operations, formed with
such secrecy and determined perseverance, were
nearly complete,' to find himself suddenly betrayed by some of his coadjutors and apparent
friends, M..l.., and R..m..l, &c. He was
consequently arrested by order of the directory
of the French Republic, under the sanguinary
Robespierre, &c. at Paris, A D. 1796, and
thrown into prison; where, in consequence of
the sentence of a military tribunal, he was confined five years and a half in irons, deprived of
what remained of his property, and finally
condemned to death; constantly expecting to

77

be led to execution: yet meanwhile experiencing every kind of misery, during this horrid confinement. The immense sacrifices my father had made, he did not regret or regard, but eagerly longed for fresh opportunities of displaying his zeal and loyalty to his Sovereign. I cannot omit the insertion of the Count D'Escar's account of these circumstances; which is literally as follows: " The Baron de Poly, " who was employed in the agency which the " king had at Paris, was, through the treachery " of the chiefs his coadjutors of that agency, of " which he would by no means partake, im- " prisoned, condemned to death, and doomed " to suffer every kind of vexation for upwards " of five years and a half with unshaken fidelity." Two of his companions died at Cayenne, a third enjoyed his liberty, by sacrificing the interests of his master, whom he betrayed, to which the Baron de Poly would never in the slightest degree accede; although arrested and imprisoned five different times, having in the whole suffered more than seven years imprisonment for his adherence to his Sovereign.

For more than two years no intelligence could be obtained by our family, of the fate of my father; although during this long period of anxiety and dread, every means were used to effect this purpose. At length he was found by his disconsolate wife, imprisoned in the dungeon of la Pelagie, loaded with irons, and suffering every kind of misery and privation; being in the most wretched condition, having only prison allowance to subsist on; almost without clothes, and no fire allowed him, even in the most inclement season; suffering in addition every species of vexation, that the malice of his enemies could devise: yet enduring all with undaunted firmness and determined resolution.

It was with the utmost difficulty permission could be obtained to see him in his dungeon; at length, however, after repeated solicitations, it was granted to my mother, who eagerly embraced the opportunity of visiting her unfortunate husband, in his miserable situation: but the reality of his present sufferings so far exceeded any thing she could have imagined, that her affliction was extreme; her immediate attention was turned to soothe the horrors of his imprisonment, alleviating as much as possible his sufferings, administering to his necessities as far as practicable, sharing as long as permitted his confinement, to soften by her presence as far as lay in her power, his miserable destiny.

The feelings of regret and horror at this first meeting, may be more easily conceived than described; the mind seemed overpowered by the weight of affliction and misery; destitute of money or friends, who feared to incur the risk perhaps of sharing his confinement, if they hazarded even a temporary visit in his dungeon, where relief seemed almost inaccessible.

My mother was persuaded to take her two sons (by her former husband) to Mons, and place them under the care and protection of Monsieur Dumez, their uncle, who resided there; he having no other family than an only son, who emigrated to England with the Count D'Artois; and returned with his Royal Highness at a subsequent period, to the residence of his father, with whom he still remains. The principal object of my mother's journey to Mons, was to collect as much of our property in specie and other valuables, as could be had on this emergency She immediately returned back to Paris, took apartments in La Rue de la Clef Faubourg St. Marçeau, and again renewed her applications to visit her husband daily in his confinement ; which, under certain restrictions, she was allowed.——This afforded me the means of access to my parent in his gloomy dungeon ; and of administering some little consolation to him in his sufferings. I was placed at a school near the prison, that I might the oftener attend him ; carrying daily some provisions for him in my pockets, in which I was instructed to use the greatest caution, not to give any ground for suspicion ; or even this small relief would have been peremptorily denied him ; and which a susceptible mind will readily conceive would have much increased our aggravated sufferings ; which were already wound up to the highest pitch, and were almost too great to bear, without giving ourselves up to despair ; but despair was happily banished, by our placing our whole trust only in the Supreme Being, whose inscrutable dictates are beyond mortal comprehension ; and by relying on the divine mercy, for the consummation of those things which we could not fathom, and for the completion of which human efforts seemed to avail but little.

My mother, notwithstanding incessantly employed herself in obtaining the best possible information how to proceed, ultimately to

obtain the so much desired object,—the liberation of my dear father: numberless ineffectual
efforts were made; and after repeatedly visiting those persons whose influence might perhaps by her frequent applications, be interested
in his behalf, the only point she could gain
in these interviews with them, was merely a
suggestion, or vague opinion; that if a petition was presented to Bonaparte in person,
perhaps some alleviation of my father's sufferings might be obtained; provided suitable opportunities were watched for, in presenting it,
and a time, if possible, was selected, when his
mind was not ruffled by any untoward event;
as it would under such circumstances, inevitably fail of the intended effect: perhaps not
only for the moment, but for the future; which
consequently ought most carefully to be regarded: and indeed required very judicious
management, to be attended with the desired
success.

How to ascertain this circumstance, my poor
mother was at a loss to conceive; nothing in
her power was omitted, or any sacrifice she
could make deemed too great to effect it: but
a considerable time elapsed before a favorable
opportunity occurred, when a petition was
presented, the most minute particulars recommended to her, cautiously attended to, and
sanguine hopes entertained of a beneficial
result; which were completely illusive, though
consolatory for the moment; they were, however, fondly cherished during the short period
of uncertainty which elapsed, before its fate
was known: but it completely failed of
success.—Several other petitions were at dif-

ferent periods presented, which terminated as
in the former instance : so that there now remained scarcely a hope of effecting it by any
means in our power. Great pains had been
taken with me, by my dear mother, to instruct
me in the most minute particulars to which I was
to attend : and at the age of six years, I presented a petition with my own hand, to Bonaparte in person, and delivered to him a short
speech, which I had been taught to repeat
word for word, for a considerable time before-
hand, until I could distinctly pronounce every
syllable it contained, with the greatest ease
and regularity ; and on my knees I begged the
life and liberty of my dear father, as nearly as
I can recollect, in the following words :—

" Noble Empereur—Jetez les yeux sur un
foible enfant qui vous demande la vie de son
Père—Daignez écouter favorablement, l'humble
pétition de la Mére et de la Fille—Épargnez,
épargnez mon Pére et rendez le a son épouse
chérie qui lui tend les bras—O'Vous généreux
et bienfaisant Monarque dont le pouvoir est
grand et que la victoire accompagné, ayez
pitié d'une humble suppliante prosternée a
vos pieds ; accordez moi la liberté et la vie de
mon Pére—Ainsi vous jouirez des bénédictions
du Tout puissant et des milliers d'hommes lui
addresseront leurs priéres pour qu'il vous
accorde Sante, bonheur, prosperite dans le
monde et la felicité des Justes dans l'autre."

The following is a translation :—

" Most noble Emperor ! behold an helpless
infant supplicating from your hands the life of
her father ! Receive the humble petition of the
Mother and Daughter :—and spare, oh ! spare

G

my father! And restore him to the arms of
conjugal affection. You, most noble Emperor, who are great in power and victorious
in arms, regard your humble suppliant! and
bless me with the liberty and life of my
honoured parent.—So shall you enjoy the
blessing and favour of the Almighty, and the
prayers of thousands shall be offered up for
your health, happiness, and prosperity."

To describe the sensations of mingled joy
and gratitude that filled my infantine breast,
when I had reason to hope, from the gracious
manner my petition was received, a successful
termination, my pen is inadequate; I can only
say, I felt such serene heavenly joy, that I can
in no way make known.

My dear father's life was spared, and proper
orders issued for his liberation, as soon as the
regular forms and necessary documents were
made out for this purpose, which were soon
completed: but not to complete our happiness:—for we were again doomed to a disappointment, wholly unforeseen by us; for such
were the anxious wishes of his companions in
captivity to gain their liberty, that all my
efforts were foiled, by one of them taking the
advantage, and obtaining his release; having
by interest procured the insertion of a description of his own person, age, stature, &c. in the
order issued for my father; and by this means,
however unjust, obtained his liberation, at the
expence of my parent's protracted confinement.
This deception, which was not detected until
too late to be remedied, at once crushed all
our hopes, and we were again plunged from
the height of human happiness, produced by

the expectation of seeing my father delivered from his long and painful imprisonment, into the greatest despair.

A considerable time now elapsed in waiting for a favorable opportunity, but there was no alternative; and we were obliged to wait with patience. Dreadful indeed was our disappointment; the anxious state of suspense we were placed in, exceeded description: every exertion was used, every interest employed, that could give us the slightest glimmering of hope; every means we could suggest resorted to, but all our efforts for the present proved of no avail.

Many other persons were placed in still more dreadful situations. I shall mention one instance.—A young nobleman was arrested by the agents of the police, at the time he was on the point of marriage with a young lady in the neighbourhood; the moment after his arrest, she took post horses, and thus arrived at Paris sometime before him; she met the cart to which he was chained, at the entrance of the capital, watched it to the prison, where her lover was destined to lie, until his execution: she then hired a lodging opposite, and communicated to him by signs, the result of her interviews with his merciless judges. All her efforts to save him proved ineffectual, and she was destined to see him perish on a scaffold. From that moment she became deranged; she retired from the fatal spot, and sought those scenes, where once she had known happiness, which she had fondly imagined would be lasting. Alas! how soon obliterated for ever:— nothing can exceed the misery and despair depicted on her countenance, one of the most interesting ever beheld; but from this fatal period, she never after recovered her senses.

My mother's anxieties were now wound up to the highest pitch, and we were determined to make another attempt as early as a favorable opportunity occurred, when I again appeared before Bonaparte in person, once more to solicit my poor parent's release. I was instructed to relate to him, in the most candid manner, the artifices used, so unwarrantably, to annul his former grant; representing the protracted suffering and misery of our whole family, from this melancholy circumstance; which I did in the best manner I was able, and had the pleasing satisfaction to observe there was some hope of ultimate success. After ascertaining the accuracy of my statement, which occupied some time, I was made happy by his renewing the order for the Baron's liberation; which we took great care should not be foiled as in the former instance.

I had surely made my application at the most propitious moment: this was indeed the happiest instant of my whole life; to be made by divine Providence the instrument of saving my dear father's life, and rescuing his person from his dreadful imprisonment, was to me a scource of the purest delight, of which my dear parents equally partook. We all returned our most fervent thanks, and addressed our silent prayers to that Omnipotent Being, whose mercy could alone have occasioned this miraculous deliverance.

A peremptory order was received previously

to my father's release from prison, for him to leave the kingdom within a short stipulated period ; and to which we were extremely glad to accede. On our arrival at Avesnes, the first object of my parent's care, was to place me under the direction and tuition of Monsieur Joseph Rosignol, minister of the altar, who resided there ; under an agreement duly signed by the respective parties.

My mother learned with the deepest sorrow on her arrival here, that her son Louis Dumez de Rilly, had been sent to the army as a conscript, by his uncle, under whose protection he had been placed ; to save his own son from this service ; as no substitute could be procured at this period, without expending a very considerable sum of money ; the young men having been so much drained by the incessant calls of Bonaparte, for such immense numbers of fresh conscripts, or as he emphatically called them, " more food for cannon ;" who were continually ordered to join his armies : and melancholy to relate, we were at this time unable to ascertain any particulars relative to his future destiny. My elder brother was induced from this circumstance, to leave the school at Mons ; and formed an acquaintance with a female, unsanctioned by his parents ; her father and mother from interested motives, did all in their power to induce him to come and live in their family, who from his youth was easily persuaded to do so ; and after a time took up his abode with them, in consequence of which, the illicit acquaintance with their daugher was continued. This family lived in the neighbourhood of one of the estates belonging to my mother,

at a village called Momiguies; they were
obliged to labour hard for a living, being very
poor and having a large family.

My father and mother used every means in
their power, persuasive and even coercive, to
induce my brother to break off this objectiona-
ble connection, but without effect; and all
their efforts proved abortive. At length they
were married, when all opposition of course
ceased. My mother gave him his share of the
property arising from the small part rescued
from the confiscation, as before related.

My mother's feelings were again much
agonized, by the information she received that
her aunt, the Mother Abbess of the order
of *Poor Clares*, was dead; and that her sister
Nettalie, who had been placed under her protection in this convent, for the reasons before
stated, had married Monsieur Du Rutz; that
they resided on one of her estates at Douai;
and that they had suffered very heavily from the
numberless requisitions and exactions of the
revolutionary government, large sums of money having at different times been expended,
to save their son from the conscription, or what
may be justly termed, the military massacre; that
they had been almost ruined by forced requisitions; the quartering on them, and support-
ing of the military, to which all were compelled,
by the tyranny of the then leading members of
the existing government.

My brother-in-law received from my parents
a sufficient sum of money to pay Mr. Joseph
Rosignol (as per agreement) at stated periods,
all the expences of my board, education, cloth-

ing, &c. for a number of years; for the due performance of which, a regular contract was drawn up and duly signed, in the presence of a Notary Public.

At the church of St. Nicholas, at Avesnes, I was baptized, by the Rev. Monsieur Bonnaire, grand Curé Diocesan of this place, in the diocese of Cambrai,; John Baptiste Pierrard was my godfather, and Mademoiselle Constance Pieu my godmother.

After the completion of this necessary duty, my parents were obliged to leave the kingdom, *1801* the time limited for their departure being nearly expired; having scarcely time sufficient to reach the frontiers within the period. My father, however, reached his native soil, Germany, in safety; but being without any employ, or certain means of subsistence, he travelled to different parts of the country, without any determinate object at that time in view: wandering from place to place, as yet uncertain of his future destination, until he resolved to quit his native country, and sail for England.

I was wholly unacquainted with these circumstances at the time, and remained in the greatest uncertainty, daily expecting to see my parents; but after repeated inquiries, I at length learnt that they were no longer at Avesnes: and when farther concealment was deemed unnecessary, I was informed of the absolute necessity for their leaving the country, and that they had not a moment's time to see me previously to their departure.

My affliction was so great, on being made acquainted with this circumstance, not knowing the destiny of my parents, who had left the country; but for what foreign kingdom I could not tell; that I at once concluded they were lost to me for ever; and in all probability I should never have the happiness of seeing them more.—This preyed so much on my mind, that every kind of indulgence was resorted to, to assuage my grief. I had permission to visit my godfather and godmother at all times, as often as I chose; as likewise other respectable acquaintances in the town; of which permission I frequently availed myself: but it was a long time before I could in any great degree relieve my anxieties. My friends tried every means they could suggest, to efface the remembrance from my mind; but in every kind of amusement, the idea of my being left as it were without parents, to watch over my youth, uncertain of their fate, or even of their being in existence, at all times so agonized my mind, that I remained long inconsolable.

A chamber in the school was furnished for me, with every thing necessary for my instruction or amusement, and a large quantity of wearing apparel, (sufficient for me for several years,) purchased for my use, by my dear mother previously to her leaving Avesnes. All these kind attentions in some measure softened my afflictions, and I became at length more reconciled to my situation; which would have been very agreeable to me, had my dear parents been permitted to reside in the town or neighbourhood; or even had I been certain of their welfare: for had I only heard from them, it would have been highly pleasing to me, and would have removed that doubt and antici-

puted dread, of which I was continually thinking:—but this consolation I could not receive;
though a glimmering of hope that I should
soon hear from them, or perhaps see them
again, kept my mind at times more at ease.—
This, however, was but of short duration, as
are most of these creations of fancy.

An unexpected and melancholy event now
occurred, which in its consequences was a
most unfortunate circumstance for me.—The
clergyman under whose care and protection I
had been placed for tuition, died before I had
been six months under his direction. I was
now doomed to suffer every calamity; and
great reason I have had to deplore his loss,
having constantly received such kind attentions
from him, until this awful period: his memory,
therefore, I shall ever revere.

My brother-in-law, on hearing of the death
of my preceptor, removed me from the school;
promising that every attention and care in his
power should be paid to me. Having married
a person contrary to the express wishes of his
parents, he for this reason never visited any of
our relations. He had at this time two children, a son and a daughter. His wife, regard-
less of my interest or welfare, used every artifice
to prejudice the mind of her husband against
me; and being more anxious to assist her own
family and relations, than to protect me, she
distributed many articles of my wearing apparel
to her own children and relations. My brother-in-law being naturally of a generous, easy,
and free disposition, assisted her family and
relations to the utmost in his power: and had
one of her sisters living with them, to help his

*[handwritten note:] in law is used as equivalent to step-broth
ling to French custom.*

wife in her domestic concerns ; but I had not been there many months, before I was made a complete drudge to the family ; in nursing the children, and doing all kind of work, which my age would lead them to expect from me. From this time my education was totally neglected, and no concern whatever entertained for my improvement or benefit.

My brother wholly unacquainted with business, was advised to turn farmer : and as he was quite a novice in this new line of business, he employed his wife's relations to cultivate his land, &c. who, in consequence of his not having a competent knowledge in agriculture, betrayed him, very shamefully, in stocking and working his farm ; so that after a year's trial, he found it quite impossible to keep on this concern : it was, therefore, after much useless toil and labour, abandoned. My brother now turned his attention to building, erected a brick-kiln, to make his own bricks; in this undertaking he met with no better success, even after he had given it a longer trial than the former, and was ultimately obliged from the self-same cause to relinquish it.

No tidings from my father having been received since he left the country, and a groundless report, moreover, circulated that my dear mother was dead ; I was thus left quite unprotected. My brother's wife did not fail to take advantage of these circumstances, and persecuted me in every way she could devise ; at the same time frequently hinting, that she kept me out of charity. I was considered of course as quite defenceless, and therefore obliged to submit to every kind of menial

drudgery and indignity, which this woman
chose to inflict on me.—I was compelled to
keep their cows and sheep in the field, knitting
at the same time, from five o'clock in the morning until six in the evening, during the spring,
summer, and autumn months; and after I
returned home from this my daily employment,
I had the milk pails to clean, and not unfrequently the stables, &c.—I milked the cows,
dug the soil, planted potatoes, and, in fact, as
I became stronger, nothing was deemed too
servile or laborious to employ me in doing.
Sometimes I found this service so extremely
irksome, that I took the liberty of reasoning
with my brother-in-law on the subject, particularly on the impropriety of assigning to me such
labour at my early age, which seemed for a
time to be productive of some good effect, but
not for any long continuance. He, however,
frequently in my presence reprimanded his
wife, for her unfeeling conduct toward me,
saying, that he had her sister in the house for
the express purpose of doing the menial work,
to which she had always been accustomed :
this occasioned frequent disagreements in the
family, but his wife had such an ascendancy
over him, that it caused an alteration of very
short duration, when he was present, but none
in his absence : I generally found it in the
end productive of a much greater degree of
severity and ill treatment toward me ; so much
so, that I was in fact pleased to embrace every
opportunity of being absent from the house, in
any out-door work or employment whatever,
that my strength would allow me to perform.

One day occupied as usual in my rural

employment, I was most suddenly surprised by the appearance of a ferocious wolf; my little flock of sheep immediately dispersed in every direction, as though conscious that their mutual safety consisted in the most precipitate flight from their dreaded enemy, who instantly pursued those nearest him; at which I must confess I was much terrified; I had, however, sufficient presence of mind to blow a horn at the instant so violently, that I had the satisfaction to hear all the others in the same employ in the neighbourhood, follow my example; and in a very short time, I was relieved from the dread and horror I experienced at the sight of this ferocious animal; by the appearance of a considerable number of peasants and labourers, properly armed, to attack, and if possible, to destroy this scourge of the neighbourhood:—for every one who guards flocks in this part of the country, is supplied with one of these horns to be sounded on such occasions only.—They succeeded in preventing the destruction of any of my sheep, but were unable to effect the destruction of the wolf.

The wolf being disappointed of his prey by their presence, immediately fled before his pursuers, and made good his retreat to the forest; to the great regret of these good people, who anxiously hoped to have been able to have prevented his retreat thither, and ultimately to have succeeded in destroying him.

Well knowing we should be continually liable to his future depredations, while prowling in search of food in the forest, these resolute peasants followed the wolf into the thickest part

of the forest, to discover if possible, his den
or retreat; but without effect, all their exertions were in vain, and they were obliged, although with much reluctance, to relinquish the
pursuit, and the hopes of reward for his destruction; thereby leaving all of us in the constant dread of future depredations from this
ferocious animal. We were not altogether
void of fear for the safety of our persons,
deeming it very probable that he might attack
the guardians, as well as the flocks they
watched; which might ere long be the case;
at least our fears inclined us to believe so.

It took me a long time again to collect the
whole of my little flock together, which the appearance of the wolf had so suddenly dispersed;
but after much trouble (added to the agitation
of my mind at the time, which in some measure
retarded it,) I at length succeeded, and returned home safe with them all; to the no
small joy of myself and friends, who long
before my return had been informed of the
circumstances of the attack on my flock, and
naturally expected some of the sheep must
have fallen a prey to this prowling enemy:
their satisfaction was much increased, when
informed that not one of them was lost. They
endeavoured to relieve my apprehensions for
the future safety of myself and flock, as much
as possible; but could not wholly remove my
fears.

It is usual for the shepherds in this part of
France, when their flocks are kept out in the
fields during the night, to remain with them in
a small wooden hut (not larger than is necessary
for the shepherd, his dog, and gun,) and made

moveable by being placed on four very low wheels; the dog is trained for the purpose, and never fails to give notice by growling or barking when any wolf approaches near the enclosure in which the flock is penned. The shepherd on the first alarm, immediately discharges his musket, then reloads it, and prepares to repel any attack, or prevent the wolves from committing any depredations; and with his faithful companion, his wolf dog, whom he releases, he goes round the enclosure. It often requires the utmost vigilance to prevent the ferocious attacks of these animals, particularly so very late in the autumn, when not unfrequently several of these hungry animals coming in droves from the forest, make their attacks at the same time conjointly. The ravages committed by them during the winter, are sometimes most distressing; the more severe the weather, particularly if much snow has fallen, and a continued frost succeed, they are then driven by hunger to commit every kind of ravage on the defenceless flocks, that happen not to be properly secured from their desperate attacks. At such times incredible mischief is done by them to the flocks and herds; they do not confine themselves to seizing the innocent sheep alone, but every domestic animal: the horse, the cow, or any other within their reach, are oftentimes destroyed by them.

It is a great happiness that England is free from these nightly depredations; for I must candidly confess that I was by no means free from apprehension when at times employed in the forests of France, in cutting grass for the cattle, in picking up rotten wood for fuel, and in collecting it into bundles to carry home on my back. These burthens were frequently so large, that I could with difficulty walk under them. At other times I was employed to pick up the dead leaves which fell from the forest trees, and which were used for litter, in the winter months, for the cattle. I likewise collected the beach leaves, for the purpose of stuffing mattresses for beds; the beech nuts I picked up in large quantities, to extract oil from them; likewise acorns for food for the swine, and if more were collected than were sufficient for our own use, they were sold to others. The wild raspberries and strawberries I likewise gathered in the woods, for to sell; and corn salad, dandelion, &c. for salads for the same purpose, without deriving the smallest gratuity or emolument to myself.

My sister-in-law had a relation who made brooms for sale; I was therefore frequently sent to cut the brushwood, and prepare it ready for his use. These unsuitable employments were continued a long time; but my brother-in-law being of a very fickle unsettled disposition, again changed his plan, and undertook the management of a mill; having a plantation on the estate, he made purchases of horses, cows, sheep, &c. and employed several servants. I always assisted in hay-making and harvest work; likewise in going round the neighbourhood with a horse, to almost every house, to sell his flour, and to collect the empty bags, and to bring them with the orders I received, back to the mill. Sometimes I was sent out to pick hops for the use of the family, and when my time was not wholly employed in out-door work, I filled up the interval by cooking, &c. for the family.——I was frequently required to drive the cattle to market to sell, and often left by my brother-in-law to mind them there, during his absence on other business in the town, which I have been obliged to do for hours at a time.

It being deemed necessary at this time to remove the plantation, I was occupied in digging the soil, carrying the young trees to other fields, and in planting them, and to collect the broken branches to make into faggots for fuel. These alterations had scarcely been completed before my brother-in-law became tired of this new concern, which like his former ones was soon abandoned.——He then removed to Fontenelle, to another mill belonging to him; he here commenced making great improvements, enlarging the house, and purchasing a quantity of inferior land, expecting by tillage and industry, to improve the soil and render the land serviceable for sowing corn and other grain.——I was occupied for a considerable length of time by assisting in filling up the ponds with earth and rubbish, and to work in the garden, to plant, sow, and weed it, to gather the fruit when ripe, and to take the children a considerable distance to school ; to churn the butter, and make the cheese ; to collect small debts from individuals, living in the neighbouring towns and villages, which was often a very tedious employment.

I was one day sent by my brother-in-law to receive some rents due to him at a distance of more than seven leagues from home, in the most inclement season of winter. I had not

reached many miles on my journey, before a
very heavy fall of snow came on ; in consequence of which the roads became almost im-
passable in many places. I soon missed my
way, and in my endeavours to recover the
road, I unfortunately fell into a pool of water,
which from being lightly frozen over was co-
vered with snow ; consequently I was almost
frozen before I could extricate myself, being so
benumbed by the intense cold, that it was
sometime before I could reach the bank ; and
after more than an hour's exertion, I escaped from
this perilous situation, and I may say imminent
danger of losing my life ; and even then I was
so much exhausted from cold and fatigue, that
it was with the greatest difficulty I proceeded
to a cottage, not far distant from this place.
On my arrival I was unable to speak, but my
cries and moans at length were heard by the
cottagers, which soon procured me admittance,
and prompt relief was afforded, which in some
measure diminished my dreadful sufferings. I
was immediately placed in a bed, and remained
with them the remainder of the day and night,
and was much recovered from the effects of the
intense cold by the morning, from the great
care and attention paid to me by these friendly
people, (although a total stranger, and wholly
unknown to them at the time,) who would not
suffer me to go alone when I left them, but sent
a person to conduct me to Chimay. When I was
sufficiently recovered so as to be able to speak,
I informed these humane people of the object
of my journey, my name, and from whence I
came ; who redoubled their kindness from motives of gratitude for past benefits, which they
acknowledged to have received from my dear

H

parents, some years prior to this accident, and seemed perfectly happy to render every assistance in their power to the child of their former benefactors.

I have thought it was a great mercy I fell into such good hands on this occasion, or it might probably have cost me my life.

When I arrived at Chimay with my conductor, the people there would not permit me to return until the following market-day, it being deemed unsafe for me to venture earlier. I was then placed under the care of some persons who were going to the market, with suitable directions that every care should be taken of me, and a severe reprimand communicated to my relations, for exposing me to such imminent danger of perishing from the inclemency of the weather, in so long a journey on foot, and particularly at such an unseasonable period of the year. This reprimand for a short time had its due effect, but was soon after forgotten, and I became gradually exposed to their usual ill treatment.

My brother-in-law was frequently engaged in law suits, and of course obliged to employ a solicitor. I was often sent with orders from this person for the payment of different sums of money, to places at a considerable distance, and not unfrequently compelled in an evening on my return, to cross the forest, without any other sustenance than a piece of dry bread, which I carried in my pocket; liable to accidents of every kind, in these gloomy woods on the approach of night, but which I providentially escaped, though I continually experienced much dread on these occasions, from which I could never wholly divest myself, when necessity obliged me to traverse them at a late hour. It was customary with my brother-in-law to send me out with quantities of cheese, which had been previously sold to his customers. I carried them in a basket on my back, to the houses of the purchasers, frequently some miles distant. I was employed also in selling his butter and eggs, at market, in fact every kind of menial work and drudgery was my constant employ, and yet I could seldom give satisfaction (do what I would) to my unreasonable relations, at any time.

If my sister-in-law ever discovered me in conversation with any respectable person, who appeared to take notice, to pity, or seemed inclined to relieve my miseries, I was sure to experience her resentment, and consequent ill treatment. Frequently on these occasions she would severely beat me, without any real cause of offence; she would never allow me, (if she could by any means prevent it) to mention my name, or that of my parents, to any person; her cruelty has been carried on several occasions to such an extreme, that I have been obliged to make my escape from her. In the absence of my brother-in-law she always selected the opportunity of inflicting on me the most severe punishments she could devise: every person in the vicinity pitied my deplorable and defenceless condition, without knowing even my real name, or family connections, merely from the great severity of treatment I continually experienced from this most unfeeling and inconsiderate woman, whose chief delight

H 2

seemed to be to increase my miseries. In my
unprotected state, 1 had no other means of preventing it, than by making my escape if possible ; at other times I had not this opportunity,
I was then obliged to submit to whatever mode
of punishment she chose to inflict on me.

My brother-in-law finding his affairs still in a
very unsatisfactory state, again changed his
employment, became an innkeeper, and took
the concern of the Red Cross inn, at Fontenel,
I was there employed to wait on his customers,
and as usual to do every kind of menial work.
It was not long, however, before he became
again dissatisfied with his new business, it being
equally unsuccessful with his previous employment, for nothing seemed to prosper that he undertook ; at least nothing was so productive as
he anticipated it would be. This new concern
was therefore quickly abandoned. His next ar-
rangement was to build himself a cottage in
the same village, and consequently he once
more turned his attention to agriculture, but
confined his views for the present, within a narrow compass, taking only a small farm, which
he hoped to be able to manage more successfully himself, without the aid of so many
helpers, to whom he had sufficient reason to
expect he might in a great measure attribute
his former ill success in this line of occupation,
as they understood but imperfectly the proper
management of land, nor did he himself know
much of this business ; but still he had gained
some little experience by his former attempts,
although these were unsuccessful. I of course
returned to my former employ, as soon as a few
cows and sheep had been purchased, and the

necessary implements, &c. again provided. The children were likewise not unfrequently left under my care the whole day, while my brother's wife was spending her time in visiting her reputed friends and relations. On her return home late in the evening, I have been often obliged to go to the forest to collect wood for fuel for the next day's consumption in the family, which required no small quantity, as nothing but rotten wood was burnt, no coal being used at any time, in consequence of the opportunity of getting wood from the forest without incurring any expence, but it was at all times with the greatest reluctance I did it in the evening, from the unconquerable trepidation and fear I continually experienced on these occasions, which had no effect on the obduracy of my sister-in-law ; I was therefore obliged to obey, and console myself as well as I could.

My education had now been totally neglected from the time I was taken from the school at Avesnes, not having had the least instruction since that period, what little I had there acquired, was nearly effaced from my memory, and comparatively lost for want of practice and due attention on the part of my relatives, who could place their own children at school, and even employed me to take them there, without ever giving me an opportunity of improvement, which most ungenerous conduct I have daily to regret; assured that I shall never be able to the extent of my wishes, to retrieve this loss of time in my youth, from the unjust and perhaps most parsimonious conduct of my careless relations, with whom I resided.

My life became so thoroughly embittered by the miseries I continually experienced that I formed the resolution (let what would be the consequence) to leave this insupportable bondage, the first favorable opportunity that presented itself, which design I carefully kept within my own breast, conscious that it would be prevented if known. I frequently called when employed in nursing the children, on an industrious old woman, who although very poor, gained a living with her family, by spinning flax very fine, for the purpose of making cambric and lace. I endeavoured to learn to spin, in this family, every few minutes I could possibly spare, until at length I could spin tolerably fine, and after considerable practice at different times, found I could manage very well. I then requested this poor woman to let me come and live with her; her husband was a day-labourer, having one son and one daughter living with them; she agreed to my request, and I left my brother-in-law's house, to take up my residence in this poor, but industrious family, which so enraged my sister-in law, that she would not give up any thing belonging to me, more than what I had at the time on my back, which were little better than rags, having been worn for such a length of time; I was in fact without any stockings, only wearing socks with my *sabots* (wooden shoes.) In this wretched plight I was cheerfully re ceived by these poor people, and every assistance in their power was afforded me : my first care was to procure, if possible, the loan of a few francs, from a gentleman in the neighbourhood, who was a manufacturer of cambric, and to whom the thread, when spun, was sold.

I called on this person, and candidly related to him my artless, but melancholy tale, of the hardships and sufferings I had undergone for such a length of time, with my unfeeling relatives; and requested the indulgence of this small loan, which I would faithfully repay him; it was immediately granted, and in addition, a quarter of a pound of flax to begin with, given me at the same time, to my great satisfaction. I informed him I had quitted my brother-in-law's house, and that I was going to live in the poor woman's family, and endeavour by the most persevering industry to get my own living if possible, for the future, which I had but little doubt of effecting. The poor cottager kindly lent me a spinning wheel, and allowed me to sleep with her daughter; it was true our bed was but indifferent, consisting only of straw, yet this was of little consequence to me at the time, having been so long accustomed to every kind of hardship and privation, besides I was completely inured to fatigue, and slept as comfortably on this humble bed that I occupied, as I could possibly have done on a bed of down. I purchased, with the few shillings I had borrowed, a loaf of bread, some cheese, butter, and meat, also a box, and some bobbins for my work. With this small stock I began my new employment, generally working until a late hour in the evening, reserving a certain proportion of my gain to pay for the oil we consumed in our employment jointly; as we always used a lamp as soon as it became dusk, and frequently worked many hours after this time, to get as much done as we possibly could. We regaled ourselves at supper with potatoes roasted in the wood embers of our fire, which, with a little salt constituted our frugal meal. As soon as day-light began to appear, we gathered rotten wood from the forest, for the daily consumption of fuel for us all ; not a moment of our time was lost, for on our return, we immediately proceeded to work. —Very fortunately we had constant employ, which was not always the case with others in the same line, which of course must be a great loss to them.

When my little stock of necessaries was exhausted, I took the work I had finished to the manufacturer, and had the happiness to find I had a trifle left, after paying him the money I had borrowed, with which I procured a fresh supply, and resumed my new employ with alacrity, I may say with pleasure, as I met with the kindest treatment from these worthy people, who fortunately for me were very religious, which I considered as a great blessing, and trust it has had its due effect on my literally-speaking totally uncultivated mind. My religious duties having been as much neglected as my education, I eagerly embraced every opportunity of gaining all the information I possibly could on this most important part of my duty. I continued my new employment for three years, with indefatigable industry and perseverance, but the very low price of the article when spun so very fine, and the length of time taken up in producing any considerable quantity by my utmost exertions, prevented my acquiring more than sufficient to defray my daily expences, for food, clothing, &c. yet I was much more cheerful and happy in my present situation, being so accustomed to labour, that I found but little inconvenience in it:

I was at times much affected while I remained in this humble cottage, by the unmerited conduct of my sister-in-law, who forbid her children ever calling on me; but in spite of this prohibition, the children would sometimes come to see me, from their natural affection, in return for the little indulgencies I had at different times, while under their roof allowed them, unknown to their mother; but if it was discovered that they had paid me a visit, she never failed severely chastising them for this simple offence. I did not wish to encourage their visits, knowing it to be contrary to their parents' order: I therefore discouraged it at all times as far as I could; this however did not prevent their coming at different times, if they had any reason to hope they could do it with impunity.

The honest cottagers had an invitation one day to go to a feast in a neighbouring village, which was regularly kept once in the year, as a holiday, in innocent amusements and rejoicings; not being quite ready when they prepared to set out, I of course requested them to go on forward, and promised to overtake them. Soon after their departure, having finished my work, I accordingly followed them as quickly as I could, in the hope of soon overtaking them; and on the road met with an elderly gentleman of very respectable appearance, who entered into conversation with me, and asked me if I knew the name of the person who lived on the estate we were then approaching. I said in reply, I knew too well, to my misfortune, for it belonged to my dear mother, but now a part only belonged to my brother-in-law, and the remainder to my uncle, Du Rutz. On this information I perceived a sudden alteration in the countenance of this gentleman, who proved to be no other person than my uncle Du Rutz himself, who soon made himself known to me. He was much shocked at the recital of the hardships and miseries I had experienced, which I related to him without reserve, in as few words as possible.

After I had finished my artless tale, he took me by the hand and conducted me to the residence of Monsieur le general Despres le Polonis, at Anor, which was not very far distant. On our arrival he explained to him the dreadful situation in which I had been left, wholly unprotected by every one who ought to have been interested in my welfare ; at the same time requesting their kindest care and attention towards me. This request was immediately complied with, which filled my mind with gratitude for so sudden and unexpected a change in my favor.

I was thus at once received into the general's family as an inmate, and my former occupation wholly renounced ; the good cottagers were remunerated for their kindness to me, and received my warmest thanks for their generous hospitality, while I resided in their family.

My cousin was so much affected by the relation of my past sufferings, that she used every endeavour to make me as happy as circumstances would permit ; and made immediate arrangements for placing me at a boarding school, to remedy as much as possible the former unpardonable neglect of my education ;

but on condition I might be permitted to go every day to see her, for the purpose of being introduced to all the relations of our family, who might call at the general's house.

My uncle Du Rutz came from Douai with his son on a short visit, and soon after returned to his residence at that place. To my accidental, but most fortunate meeting with this gentleman, I am wholly indebted for my change of situation, which promised to be in every way so beneficial to me ; and I returned my most heartfelt acknowledgments to him for his humanity and great kindness to me. I felt so happy in the society I was now led into, that the time passed swiftly away, I had scarcely time to think of my former miserable state ; a continued round of pleasing amusements (after school hours) when I returned to my cousins, from the novelty of such scenes which I had previously been wholly unaccustomed to, quite delighted me ; besides, having the great satisfaction of being introduced to my relatives, and by this means becoming acquainted with them ; who all behaved in the kindest manner to me on every occasion, and seemed to take a pleasure in affording their assistance : I had only to regret that I had not earlier been fortunate enough to be introduced to this worthy family, for I had not resided here more than six months, when I received a letter from my disconsolate parents, (from whom I had not previously heard,) requesting every information from me respecting the state of my health; and a circumstantial account of particulars, relating to myself during their long absence ; requiring an immediate answer, stating that several former letters had been written to me; none of which were received. I communicated the contents of the letter to my cousin, and complied with their kind request, by replying to every particular; fully describing my former and my present situation, in the most correct manner that I was able to do; not concealing or exaggerating any circumstance. Soon afterward I received a second letter from my father, with a peremptory order to come to England, as early as possible; at the same time enclosing a sum of money to defray the expences of my journey. I of course immediately obeyed the summons, and made preparations for my departure; taking leave of all my friends, and sincerely thanking them for their very great civility and kindness to me; being naturally, extremely anxious to embrace the earliest opportunity of once more seeing my dear parents, whom I had at times conjectured were lost to me for ever.

Monsieur le general Després sent an old and very faithful servant, to accompany me to Avesnes, for the purpose of my taking leave of my godfather and godmother, with other friends and acquaintance there; which duty performed, he took a place for me in the coach, and continued the journey with me to Douai; where I paid a visit to my uncle Du Ruiz, and remained with him a few days, before I took my leave. I was much affected at this time with the melancholy situation of my poor aunt, whose mental afflictions occasioned my deepest sorrow. I acquainted my uncle with the circumstances of my journey to England, which met with his entire approbation. We then proceeded to St. Omers, having a recommendatory letter to Mr. Br.wn, who, we were informed, lived at his seat at a village called Halline, not far distant. On our arrival, the old servant of my worthy relation left me, under the care of this family, and returned according to his previous orders, back to his master at Anor.

I remained with Mrs. Br.wn nearly three months, before a safe conveyance could be found for proceeding on my journey; this kind lady interested herself much in my behalf; the family at home at this period consisted of three children, the eldest daughter became much attached to me, in fact I found kind friends in them all. Mr. Br.wn resided at Dunkirk. It was at length determined I should go there, and on my arrival take my passage on board the first vessel bound for England, that I could meet with; this scheme was no sooner suggested than I most anxiously longed for its completion, and immediately prepared for my departure, leaving my best thanks for the great kindness I had met with in this charming family; which on any other occasion I should have quitted with the greatest reluctance.

I proceeded on to my destination, and on my arrival at Dunkirk, apartments were taken for me in an English family near the residence of Mr. Br.wn, who had a large circle of friends and acquaintance in the place. I was almost daily introduced to different captains of merchant vessels, for the purpose of procuring a passage for England, but to my great disappointment, not one could be found who dared to run the risk of taking me on board his ship, not having any passport in my possession from the then existing French government, without which no one was permitted to quit the kingdom. I was therefore compelled to remain here for nearly six months longer, my parents sending me money to defray my expences until some favourable opportunity should occur to enable me to make my escape, and fortunately reach the so much wished for shores of England.

I experienced every civility and kindness in this place, many of Mr. Br.wn's friends inviting me to their houses, who kindly introduced me to their different parties; and admitting me to all the amusements of the place; they took me to the opera, concerts, &c. which were extremely agreeable to me, and in some measure relieved my mind from the great uneasiness I experienced arising from the so frequent disappointments I met with in every attempt made to effect my escape, which I really began to think was almost impossible for me to accomplish; the regulations being so very strict, it was extremely difficult to elude them.

As a final resource, I was obliged to assume the disguise of a youth, and act in some menial capacity, as the most probable way of succeeding; many stratagems of this kind were attempted, but without success; and I began to experience great uneasiness, in spite of all the gaiety and amusements of the place, which now began totally to lose their effect with me.

As the novelty of these public exhibitions in a great measure wore off, the depression of my spirits increased : I almost despaired of being able to comply with the anxious wishes of my dear parents, as the difficulties and impracti- bility of succeeding seemed to increase, rather than diminish.

At the time I was almost desponding, I for- tunately heard that a lady had arrived at one of the inns in this place, provided with the proper documents for herself and servants, and who was going to embark for England ; on receipt of this information, I lost no time in waiting upon her, although a total stranger, (yet such an opportunity was not to be allowed to escape me ;) I was immediately introduced to her, and after candidly explaining my hope- less and miserable situation, stating the many fruitless attempts I had made to effect my escape, I suggested a plan which, after some hesitation, and much entreaty on my part, was at last agreed to; although this lady was well aware of the great risk she herself ran, if detected in aiding or assisting the escape of any one ; and it was agreed upon between us that I should pass for one of her servants on board the ship. Assuredly the great interest this benevolent stranger took in my case, only could induce her to comply with my most earnest wishes, to take me even in this menial capacity.

Overjoyed at the success of my plan, I immediately made the proper arrangements : soon equipped myself suitably to my intended station ; bid adieu to all my friends, and waited on this lady as one of her attendants : our scheme was fortunately successful ; we were taken on board the ship without suspicion, it

being an American merchant vessel ; which set
sail about five o'clock in the evening; and we
arrived at Dover the following day about
eleven o'clock, it being the 2d of August, 1810 ;
to my inexpressible joy and satisfaction.

I had sometime previously to my leaving
France, been furnished with letters of recommendation from the Marquis of B.ck.ng..m,
sent to me in a packet by my dear mother, and
which were now of infinite service to me. I
was left by the lady with whom I came over in
charge of her packages and boxes, at the inn,
during the time she procured a post-chaise, to
take us on our way to London ; on her return
we took some refreshment, which appeared
very different to what I had been previously
accustomed, particularly the large size of the
joints of meat, and the very different mode of
cooking them ; which, I must confess, at that
time much surprised me. I likewise noticed
the very different manners of the people here;
but what struck my mind most forcibly, was
the apparent singularity of the language, not
knowing a word scarcely of what I heard
around me, but which seemed intelligible
enough to every one else : I figured to myself
the difficulties I should have in acquiring a
language foreign to me, and so very different
in every respect to my native tongue : amid
these momentary reflections, I recollected I
should soon have the happiness to see my dear
parents, with whom I could converse, until I
had acquired some knowledge of the English
language ; this reconciled me completely : and
we were soon ready to proceed on our journey.
We entered the vehicle which was waiting for

us, and proceeded at a rate we are but little accustomed to in France. We arrived in town early on the third day, which greatly delighted me. I had spent very uneasy nights at the inns, having been unable to close my eyes the whole time, principally arising from my great anxiety and perturbation of mind; being so overjoyed in the anticipation of the pleasure I should experience, in once more beholding my long-lost and ever dear parents.

My first object on my arrival in London was to find out the bank of Messrs. Br.wn, C.bb, & Co. to make inquiry respecting Mr. Br.wn, son of the lady with whom I staid at Halline, in France; I had letters of recommendation to him, and was so fortunate as to meet with him here.—On being introduced to this gentleman, my first inquiries were relative to my father and mother; to whom, I had inconsiderately though fondly indulged the hope, I should be immediately introduced: but what was my surprise and disappointment, when informed I could not possibly see them at present; though a promise was held out to me, that I should soon have that satisfaction; but that as they did not reside in London, some little time must elapse before they could be made acquainted with my arrival in England, and a day or two more before they would reach town.—1 was then informed that they resided at Middleton-Cheney, in Northamptonshire, a distance of nearly eighty miles from me. I was therefore obliged to wait with patience, and console myself with the certainty of seeing them in a few days. The lady, my companion in our journey, now took her leave of me, to whom I

I

returned my most grateful thanks. Mr. Br.wn
shortly after conducted me to his residence; I
remained in this gentleman's family two or
three days, who immediately wrote to my
parents, communicating to them the welcome
intelligence of my arrival at his house; after
which I communicated all the news I was
commissioned with from his mother; and endeavoured to conceal the anxiety of mind I
laboured under at my disappointment, in not
being able immediately to see my dear parents:
this, however, did not escape Mr. B's. observa-
tion; and for the purpose of diverting my mind
a little from this object, he proposed a visit to
the lady, with whom I made my escape from
France. This certainly had in some measure
the desired effect for a time; after which, he
took me to an immensely (in appearance to
me) large brewery, shewing and describing to
me every thing worthy of notice in the place;
the amazing size of the vessels, their great number, and the surprisingly large scale on which
this concern was conducted, struck me with no
small degree of astonishment, the whole being
a complete novelty to me, having never before
seen any thing of the kind; nor could I have
previously formed any adequate idea of the
magnitude of such concerns, without ocular
demonstration. I was much pleased with this
visit, which occupied some considerable time.
On our return, Mr. Br.wn was obliged to leave
me for a short time, having business of importance to transact in the city. During his absence, I amused myself as well as I could, by
noticing the number and bustle of the persons
continually passing and repassing in the street,
which appeared very amusing to me. On the

third day, during the absence of Mr. Br.wn, a hackney coach stopped at the door, I saw an elderly lady and a venerable old gentleman alight; and I was much at a loss to conjecture who these visitors could be. From what innate cause I was not at the moment aware: I was on the tiptoe of expectation, but could not for one moment conceive that this apparrently elderly woman and gentleman could possibly be my parents, there being to me such evident disparity in their age and persons, from what I recollected of them when they left me in France. I remained sometime in anxious suspense; at length Mr. Br.wn returned, and the mystery was soon elucidated, by his immediately introducing the lady to me as my mother; the elderly gentleman who accompanied her was Monsieur de Chevalier de Calbiac, a French gentleman, and intimate friend of our family. I was so overcome by the sudden joyful sensations that all at once rushed into my mind, that for a time I could scarcely articulate my words, to express my gratitude to him for having, at so unexpected a moment restored me to one of my dear parents: yet I could not restrain my surprise at seeing my dear mother appear so very old, and so much altered in her person and appearance: but this mystery was soon developed by being informed that the evident alteration in her health and person, principally arose from grief and misfortunes, of which she had experienced so large a share, since leaving me at Avesnes, arising from the loss of her property and dear relatives, in fact, miseries of the most poignant kind; the detail of which, might here be deemed superfluous.

I 2

After remaining at Mr. Br.wn's a few hours, we accompanied Monsieur de Calbiac to his residence, and staid with him nearly three weeks. We waited on the Duke de Lachat, Ambassador from France, who was so much afflicted at the recital of the miseries and misfortunes of our family, that he frequently shed tears of regret at this interview, and promised to exert his influence in our behalf. We then proceeded to the town residence of the Marquis of B.ck..g..m, who was unfortunately not in town at this time: our next visit was to Richard Lorentz, Esq. the German Ambassador, from Hesse Cassel, from whom we met with a very flattering and kind reception; and received a promise that his best exertions should be used, in promoting the interest of our family. We then proceeded to the Emigrant Office, and there met with great civility from Joseph Parkinson, Esq. who afforded us all the necessary information we required. We next called on Madame la Comtessè de Callone, Monsieur L'Abbé Madline, Monsieur L'Abbé Robert, and several other distinguished friends of my parents; from all of whom we met with the greatest kindness and sympathy. We next called on an old servant of our family, whose name was Le Clerc; my mind indeed was very forcibly affected at this interview, on finding that his daughter, who was present, had received a tolerably liberal education, and had even made some proficiency in music; she played us several tunes on the harp and piano, delightfully: which made me feel most poignantly the irretrievable loss I had sustained, by the unpardonably cruel neglect of my education, from the time I lost my late worthy ecclesiastical preceptor, until I had the happiness to be introduced to the family of the general Despres, at Anor; and I much regretted having been able to remain there so short a time. Some days after we called on Madame Courtois, and on Monsieur C.ss.n, who was uncle to an unfortunate youth, whose name was Francis Senage, whom my father and mother had agreed to take under their care and protection for seven years, on condition of annually receiving a small stipulated sum, and which his uncle usually paid, towards his board, maintenance, clothing, &c.

After we had finished all we had to do of any importance in town, we took our places in the coach for Banbury, and returned to Mr. Calbiac's to take our leave of him. At the time appointed we proceeded to the coach office, and soon commenced our journey for Oxfordshire; my father being apprised of our coming, met the coach on our arrival, and conducted us to Middleton-Cheney. I now felt completely happy, in being once more united in the same family with my dear parents; who equally sympathised with me in this so long wished for event : the general satisfaction, however, was soon much damped, by their being in such distressed circumstances, which unfortunately I had not the power in any way to relieve; but had the melancholy prospect before me, of perhaps still adding to their burthen, by my presence; we, however, consoled ourselves with the hope, that something might in the course of time, turn up to our advantage in this respect, to make our lives less grievous in future.

I detailed to my afflicted parents more fully the accumulated miseries and great distress I had experienced during their absence, from those relations, who should have endeavoured to alleviate or prevent them. At this recital of my misfortunes, their affliction was extreme; more particularly on the total neglect of my education, which in its consequences, was irremediable. This unpardonable neglect was doubly grievous to them, having at the time, taken every precaution that human foresight could suggest; as they did not expect at the time of our separation, it would have been for so many years: yet even this they had, as they conceived, fully provided for, by leaving in the hands of my brother-in-law, a sum of money adequate to this purpose, under a regular agreement for its fulfilment, legally drawn up and signed by the parties; how far this had been attended to, my readers have been fully informed in the preceding part of this narrative: my parents were, literally speaking, from this cause almost overwhelmed with affliction, which I endeavoured to soften and relieve by every means in my power; but I am sorry to say with but little effect.

I anxiously wished to render myself useful in every thing I was capable of doing, assisting to the utmost in my power in the domestic, and in fact every concern in the family. My mind having been thus left uncultivated, and my religious duties much neglected, I could not be surprised at the anxious wishes of my parents, to endeavour in some measure to remedy the latter defect; accordingly the Rev. Mr. Hersent was applied to, and requested to instruct me in this most important and necessary duty, which he immediately undertook to do; and who, with the zeal of a truly worthy pastor, communicated to me all the most necessary and important duties of our religion, which I confidently trust will be eminently beneficial to me through life; to this person my most grateful acknowledgements are ever due.—The great truths of salvation this reverend gentleman enforced on my untutored mind, by so plainly elucidating them, that they have had a happy effect in numberless instances on me; and occasioned an anxious desire on all suitable opportunities, to acquire a full knowledge of every minute duty of a good christian; which it will ever be my pride and most anxious wish to persevere in, to the utmost my poor abilities will allow: earnestly hoping I shall be enabled as I number more years, to fulfil still more strictly my duty to the Omnipotent Being, from whom all blessings flow, that are experienced in this sublunary world. It seemed to be the wish of my parents, if my own inclination coincided with theirs, that after their decease I should retire to a convent, to which injunction I shall most probably at some future period accede.

In a conversation with my father, he informed me, whilst speaking of the number of emigrants in England, that he had served with distinguished honour in the regiment of veterans, composed only of emigrant French officers, in the loyalists' army: but that all their efforts were unattended with the desired success:—being always opposed by such an immense desparity of forces, they were ultimately defeated; and compelled to make the best retreat circumstances would allow; and that in order to escape, he was obliged to assume the character and occupation of a master of a manufactory of pottery; though this did not long shield him from the active scrutiny of his implacable enemies. He was eventually discovered, and thrown into prison: from which he had much difficulty to escape with life. He likewise stated to me, that he was engaged in the agency of the king, in the affairs of La Villehernois and his adherents; and was the only person out of the whole number, who miraculously escaped destruction: every one of whom, with this single exception, having perished in the good cause of loyalty to their sovereign.—And often has my parent expressed a wish, to have himself died in the field of glory.

My father enjoyed but a very indifferent state of health, after his long and painful imprisonments; which had completely undermined and ruined his constitution. for the reestablishment of which, or the restoration of temporary health, every means that suggested the least probability of relief, were tried, though in vain; nothing could be devised that was found of any real service to him; and although the advice of the most eminent physicians was consulted, it proved of no effect: a rapid decline seemed to baffle all attempts to cure; in fact, it was beyond the power of medicine to effect it. The perturbed state of my poor parent's mind, arising from his pecuniary embarrassment, increased the malady which was now making rapid advances towards terminating his earthly career.

At this period my afflicted parent was obliged to leave his cottage at Middleton-Cheney; and was by the humane interposition of Fiennes W.k..m, Esq. rescued from his most wretched situation.—This good, generous, and benevolent gentleman received the houseless wanderer into his own family, until he had prepared one of his cottages for my parents' reception: and to the last day of his existence did my father share the counsel, charity, and friendship of this most benevolent protector.—May such deeds live in the grateful remembrance of posterity, as they will never be effaced from mine, and in sweet memorial rise before the throne of grace!—Such honourable, disinterested, generous, and most humane conduct, speaks for itself in stronger language than my feeble pen can possibly convey; and my gratitude for such acts of munificence, will cease only with my existence.

I remained at this period, by desire of my parents, in the family of Mr. H.rr.s, of Overthorpe; but on their removing from Middleton, I came to Banbury, to arrange every thing in the best manner I was able in their new habitation, for their mutual comfort and convenience. I occasionally came to visit them, and regularly washed and mended the linen every week, assisting in every thing I could make myself useful in: but as my dear father's health was most rapidly declining, it was not long before he was confined to his bed, daily getting worse, although every means were resorted to, that his medical attendants could devise; but still his complaint completely baffled every attempt at removal; till at length, exhausted nature gave up the struggle, and my dear father departed this life in the fortieth year of his age, in the happy expectation of a blessed futurity.

He had conducted himself as a zealous professor of the Catholic Church, during the whole of his long and tedious illness; and frequently received the holy sacrament. His conversion from the Lutheran persuasion, and his death were very remarkable: and when he found he should soon enter into *the house of his eternity,* he received with great edification all the rites of the Catholic Church, and expired, after having communicated, on the 12th day of December, 1810, and was interred in Banbury church yard.

The Rev. Mr. M.rg.n, the Rev. Mr. R..ck, the Rev. Mr. P. Hersent, and the Rev. Mr. Ch.rt.n, visited the Baron de Poly during his illness.

F. Wy.kh.m, Esq. the Rev. Mr M.rg.n, M. W.st, and Mr. Br.ckw.ll attended the funeral; Mr. Br.ckw.ll's men carried the corpse to the grave on this solemn occasion.

I have been credibly informed, that his best friend Mr. Wy.kh.m, who esteemed and paid great respect to the Baron's memory, was the ever good Samaritan; and that with other most respectable gentleman, he acted on this as on other occasions, with private benevolence and liberality: and am happy to add the same humane conduct was afterwards continued to the afflicted widow.

Mrs. M.rg.n with anxious solicitude endeavored to mitigate my mother's sorrows, and relieve the distresses of the children of misfortune oppressed with adversity in a foreign land; and ordering what was requisite for the funeral. The Rev. Mr. M. rg. n officiated on this melancholy occasion.

The benevolent and disinterested conduct of Mr. and Mrs. W. st, at this distressing period, voluntarily affording their kind assistance in furnishing the funeral, &c. must claim my most grateful thanks; I was totally ignorant of this circumstance until a short time since, when Mrs. M. L. ng.; my most munificent benefactress and ever valuable friend, and who has afforded me a kind asylum for so long a period in her house, &c. informed me of it: for had I known it sooner, I should long since have personally expressed my gratitude to Mr and Mrs. W. st, for such benevolence.

My dear mother's grief at this momentous period was inconsolable, being herself in an extremely weak state of health, which this melancholy event much aggravated; the very embarrassed state of our affairs still further augmented it: in fact, her despondency daily seemed to increase with her malady, and could not be removed by human means.

My deceased parent's small pension of course now ceased, and we found ourselves under the distressing necessity of soon after selling the few goods and chattels, still remaining in our possession, to satisfy as far as they would go, the urgent demands of our creditors; but they produced but a very small sum indeed, toward accomplishing this desirable object.

After the sale, we removed to a small house in West-street; here our calamities increased, and we found it utterly impossible any longer to support Francis Senage, who at an early age had lost his mother.—His father, an officer in the army, had returned to France during the peace, and nothing had been heard of him since that period by us. As we did not receive the small sum agreed on for his maintenance, &c. after he had remained seven years and a half in our family, necessity obliged us to send him back to his uncle in London, after repeated applications had failed in procuring payment of the sum due to us for his support. Being wholly unable any longer to bear this additional burthen in our misfortunes, we were compelled, although with much reluctance, to resort to this mode, from actual want of the means for our own individual support.

Through the interest of the Ambassador from Hesse Cassel, and the kind assistance of our friends, with considerable difficulty my mother at length succeeded in procuring a small increase to her pension from the French government, during a limited period, which was regularly paid to, and thankfully received by us.

Frequent applications were made by friends of my mother residing in London, to persuade her to remove to town; where (should she be inclined to adopt this plan) she would be more immediately situated in the circle of her former acquaintance, which might in some degree relieve her mind from the gloom and despondency under which she laboured; yet all their kind solicitations failed, as she could not be prevailed on to accept their kind offers.

It being my mother's particular wish to remain in Banbury, and be placed in the same grave with my father, at her decease; this seemed principally to occupy her thoughts, and she frequently said that she most anxiously desired its fulfilment. Her health was gradually declining, although much relieved by the interpositions of her numerous friends; yet she never enjoyed a day's good health for a long period.

The late Michael W..dh.ll, Esq. and Mrs. Ingram were invaluable friends to my poor parents; for which most generous and humane assistance, I must beg leave to pay to them my most grateful tribute of thanks; not that any thing I can say will add to the so well known philanthrophy of these truly good persons, whose actions alone speak loudly in their praise:—my silent prayers flowing from the grateful source of benefits conferred, are frequent to the throne of grace; to that Omnipotent Being, whose all-seeing eye penetrates into the secrets of every heart, and will not reject the incense of gratitude.

Mr. and Mrs. B.ll and family were amongst the earliest friends of my dear parents, and who still continue their friendship to me; which also claims my warmest acknowledgments. Mrs. R.ss.l and family were likewise very early friends; as was also the truly benevolent Sir G..ge L.., of H..tw..l-House, who at all times kindly interested himself in softening the cares and adminstering to the relief of the afflictions of my dear parents; and whose many acts of truly christian charity, it is my consolation to believe, will be amply rewarded in futurity.

The Rev. Mr R..ck, chaplain to Br.wn M..st.n, Esq., of K..nn..gt.n, and the Rev. Monsieur P. H..ss..t, were also invaluable friends, both spiritually and temporally speaking, to my parents, and myself.

The Marquis of B..k..gh..m kindly patronized and assisted our family; and on my arrival in England, proposed taking me into his family; but my parents were so much hurt at the total neglect of my education, that they could not by any means be induced to comply with this humane request. The noble Marquis, with his usual munificence, defrayed all the expences of my journey from the continent, for which, with many other acts of kindness, my most grateful thanks are justly due;—the remembrance of such signal benefits, will be ever sacredly treasured up in my memory; and I earnestly hope will meet with an ample reward, when the vain shadows of sublunary things shall be no more.—To the Rev. Mr. Ch..t.n, I am infinitely indebted, for his very great kindness to my dear parents and myself; as likewise to the Rev. Mr. M..rg.n and family, who very kindly interested themselves as much as possible in our welfare. The late Mr. Chapman, and the present R. Br.yn., Esq. were also very benevolent and kind to us; the latter gentleman has continued his kindness to me, to the present period, and to whom I beg leave to return my most grateful and very sincere acknowledgements, for his disinterested benevolence.

T..m.thy C..bb, Esq. and family have been invaluable friends to my parents and myself; their kindness has been invariably continued;

and they have afforded me every comfort in my distresses, being ever disinterested and benevolent towards me; and invariably promoting my interest and welfare : by every practicable means :—my gratitude for such liberality will only cease with my life.

My mother, previously to leaving France, was obliged to disguise herself on her journey, as occasions required, for her own personal safety; but fortunately, after innumerable difficulties, she safely effected her escape : but at an expence she was scarcely able to bear, at this most distressing period. This circumstance was of serious consequence to her afterwards, yet the necessity of the case required these sacrifices; which it was useless to regret, as there was no possibility of avoiding it.

The accumulated distresses my parents had experienced, from the time they were obliged to quit France, my mother related to me, prior to her death, and which I shall recapitulate as nearly as possible in her own words.—On their arrival in London, she took lodgings in an obscure street of the metropolis, at as moderate a rent as possible, not having the means to provide more suitable apartments; but this was a trifling circumstance, and deemed of but little consequence. Almost unknown, and scarcely knowing any persons themselves; in a foreign country, destitute of property; without any employ, or probable means of obtaining for a time, even the common necessaries of life: this subject alone engrossed all their thoughts; and most certainly their future prospects were gloomy in the extreme, until some relief could be procured.

My mother, by mere accident, had the happiness to meet with a person, who employed her in working embroidery; this was a relief as sudden as unexpected: she invariably began her work very early in the morning, and continued at it until a late hour in the evening, to enable her to support herself and husband: who at this time could get no employ whatever: which added greatly to their misfortunes; nor could any pension for himself and family be obtained for some years after this period.

My mother at length was obliged to make list shoes for sale, platted straw for making bonnets, &c. and in fact, laboured with the most persevering industry early and late, to provide for their sustenance so indefatigably, as was truly wonderful, it being so very different from her former occupations, never before having been accustomed to any kind of labour; but necessity is the mother of invention, which enabled her to persevere even with cheerfulness in her new and laborious employment.

My mother having occasion early one morning to take some work home that she had finished, had left my father in bed, and was detained rather longer than she expected, in not immediately meeting with the person by whom she was employed at the shop.—On her return, the neighbours informed her, that during her absence her husband had very nearly been accidentally killed. On entering the house in the greatest imaginable alarm, she found that my poor parent had fallen down stairs, and broken his leg; and that he was still lying at the bottom of the staircase, in the greatest agony.— In her first moments of alarm, (from the great perturbation and distress of her mind,) my dear mother knew not what to do; but when she had recovered a little from the sudden shock, she immediately procured assistance, and had the Baron removed up stairs to his bed. The next thing which on the emergency occurred to her mind, was to write to the French and German Ambassadors, stating to them the melancholy accident that had happened; at the same time describing the very miserable situation in which they were placed; without medical assistance, or the means of procuring any; almost unknown, and destitute of money; and that they had no other resource but to apply to the well-known humanity and benevolence of these gentlemen.—Very fortunately this appeal was not made in vain: as soon as possible after they were made acquainted with these circumstances, the French Ambassador arrived, bringing with him an eminent French surgeon; the German Ambassador was but a few minutes later, and brought with him an English doctor of eminence: they both immediately proceeded to the examination of the fracture. It was the opinion of these eminent medical gentlemen, that an amputation of the leg or thigh would be necessary, from the nature of the fracture; but this was objected to by my parents, if any possible means could be devised to complete the cure without, it being a bad compound fracture, and from appearances deemed almost impractible.—However, in compliance with the anxious wishes of my afflicted parents, these medical gentlemen, with great difficulty and extreme attention on their part, ultimately effected a cure without amputation; to the great satisfaction of my distressed parents;

K

but it required a considerable length of time, before this desirable object could be effected: and the pain was most excruciating for a very long period; it being the third time the same limb had been, by different accidents, so much injured: twice in the knee, once as has been before related, and again by the kick of a vicious horse, in the same place; which occasioned the most intolerable pain for many months after: in fact, my father was seldom free for many years from acute pain in this part, although every thing that could be of benefit, or even deemed likely to be of service, was tried in vain.

This unfortunate accident was in the end productive of some good; so true it is that good frequently arises from what we deem a great evil: in this instance it was completely verified. My parents were now relieved from the accumulating distress they had so long experienced in their circumstances, by the liberal and most generous donations of several benevolent individuals; who each subscribed a certain sum towards the relief of their present embarrassment and future comfort. This most welcome relief was so opportunely afforded, and with such delicacy of friendship carried into effect, that we did not even know the names of the benefactors; a circumstance I now regret, not being able personally to pay my just tribute of praise to the humanity of these individuals; and to which they are so justly and fully entitled.—Their conduct, so similar to the good Samaritan's, cannot be too highly applauded; nor will it ever be effaced from my memory:—such worthy actions will undoubtedly meet with ample reward, when time shall be no more.

About this period, my father, being previously of the Lutheran persuasion, embraced the holy catholic faith, and was received into the catholic church by the Rev. Dennis Chaumont, director of the foreign mission in China; at this period also he experienced a sudden cessation of pain in his knee, which had for such a length of time so cruelly tormented and afflicted him, with but little previous intermission day or night.

My poor mother had at different times (previously to the receipt of the friendly donations above stated,) been obliged to sell all her ornaments of jewellery, diamond rings, &c. for their mutual support; and was at this period taken suddenly ill; which illness soon became so very serious, that for a considerable time her life was in danger, and for some time despaired of by her medical attendant; a favourable change at length took place, the violent symptoms diminished, and after a few months she in some degree recovered; but never after enjoyed a good state of health.—For some years her bodily strength had been visibly declining, but this last illness had made much more fatal inroads on her constitution, than any of her former attacks; although she had experienced such severe afflictions both in body and mind, that she was now so extremely weak and debilitated, that it required great care and some months' medical attendance, before she could be pronounced out of danger; and a much longer time before she could assist in domestic concerns.

Very fortunately my father was now nearly become convalescent, and was employed by the late Mr. P.tt, in writing for government; but this new employ was not of long duration, or at all certain, sometimes their being very little to do, at other times nothing whatever; this did not suit my father's convenience or necessity; he was therefore obliged to decline it altogether, and endeavour to procure something more regular and certain; but this he found very difficult to obtain. After innumerable attempts had failed of success, he was obliged to wait with patience, until something more favourable could be obtained.

During my mother's illness, Madame la Comtesse de Callone and family were most kind friends; likewise Madame la Baronne Defache and family: several benevolent catholic clergymen also alleviated as much as possible her acute sufferings, at this distressing period; affording spiritual and temporal relief in the most praiseworthy manner; which indeed was a great comfort and solace to her troubled mind.

Charity is the virtue which distinguishes the true ecclesiastic from his contemporaries, and without which all others are of no avail:—how truly this most necessary christain virtue was exemplified by these good pastors, is so evident, that it needs no comment.—May their future reward equal their desert. This benevolence was not only their characteristic on this occasion, but the rule of conduct adopted, and always practised by them, as far as their limited means would allow; which most fully and most unequivocally bespeaks the true Christian spirit.

My father removed to another residence, and

had a catholic chapel in one part of his dwelling house; the Rev. Mons. L'Abbé Grongelle, officiated there for a considerable time.

From the chemical and medical knowledge my father had acquired, it was recommended to him to make an essay in this profession; being quite disappointed in his expectations, and finally tired of waiting such a length of time, always in uncertainty, he adopted the plan; but it wholly failing of the expected success, the profession of medicine was abadoned; and the trade of book-seller adopted: this was likewise unsuccessful; and after many fruitless efforts ultimately relinquished.

His next attempt was in the bookbinding business, but from his imperfect knowledge of the trade, he was continually liable to the impositions of the workmen he was obliged to employ; and from this cause it was attended with no better success than his former plans Many other schemes were tried in vain, and my parents determined on leaving the metropolis; they accordingly came to reside at Banbury, in Oxfordshire, but (in the first instance) remained here but a short time; removing to a cottage in the neighbouring village of Overthorpe, in Northamptonshire.—The Baron and his lady made choice of this place, because being catholics, they wished to live in the neighbourhood of a catholic chapel: they also intended to establish a school there; this completely failed of the success anticipated: and I am extremely sorry to say, most of my father's undertakings did, but from what cause I am unable to determine.

From this place they removed to Middleton-Cheney, where they resided on my return from the continent, and for some little time afterwards, but in a very ill state of health; and were ultimately obliged to quit their cottage here, without having any place to go to. It was at this juncture the humane Mr. Wy.kh.m interposed, and placed them in a cottage of his own at Banbury, (as has been before stated in this narrative,) where we remained until the decease of my father:—sometime after, we removed to a small house in West-street.

I had proceeded thus far with my memoirs, when a letter was received from my uncle Du Rutz, now residing at Douai, communicating to me the intelligence that my brother-in-law Louis Dumez de Rilly, (with whose destiny I had been wholly unacquainted before,) was captain in the regiment of Orleans; that on his return from America, at the age of twenty-four years, he found himself immediately after his disembarkation in France, in an engagement, in which his regiment highly distinguished itself; but that he was struck by a musket ball in the arm, which having been but ill attended to in proper time, that the wound occasioned his death.

My other brother-in-law, Dumez de Rilly, is now employed as a custom-house officer, near Vervins, in France, and has a large family to maintain; but very fortunately during the present peaceable state of the country, which it is to be hoped will continue for many years uninterrupted by foreign or domestic hostilities, there is not so much difficulty to be anticipated in providing for a numerous family, as in times of commotion, tumult, and disturbance; which are generally the natural attendants on a state of war.—May heaven avert the recurrence of such an event in my native country, or in any part of Europe; not only from motives of humanity to our fellow creatures, but that by a long and happy peace, the nations may be enabled to heal the wounds, and in some measure repair the horrid ravages and immense expenditure, occasioned by the late long and tremendous conflicts; which had for so many years afflicted Europe by their desolating influence, and accumulating miseries; particularly those countries in which the seat of war happened more immediately to be experienced. —Their losses have been immense, and I should conceive almost irreparable, without a long continued state of peace and repose.

I had hitherto enjoyed almost an uninterrupted state of good health, scarcely remembering a day's illness or indisposition worthy of notice; it was, however, soon to be quite the reverse: for on Good-Friday, having gone with Madame, my mother, to the catholic chapel, at Overthorpe, during divine service an alarm of fire was heard in the village. Anxious to afford the most prompt assistance on such an occasion, we quitted the chapel and hastened to the spot. I exerted myself to the utmost in my power, in removing articles of furniture, &c. from Mr. Ch.ml.,n's, from about nine o'clock in the morning, until nearly five in the evening; carrying them in the best way I could, from Warkworth to Overthorpe, to place them in safety. Although the distance from one village to the other was not con-

siderable, yet going to and from each place so
repeatedly, with such heavy loads, some of
which I had great difficulty in carrying, I
began to feel much fatigued. Having taken
no kind of refreshment during the whole time,
great lassitude and faintness succeeded, to
which I paid but little attention, until the fire
was extinguished; after which I walked to
Banbury, and reached home unusually wearied,
which I attributed to my over exertions, continued for so many hours without intermission.
Yet I experienced sensations very different
to what I had ever felt before, from the severest
fatigue; and anxiously wished to get some
rest, fondly hoping I should be relieved by
repose, and that by the morning my distressed
feelings and bodily sufferings would be en-
tirely removed. I consoled myself with con-
sidering that my greatest exertions had been
made in the cause of humanity, and for benefiting
individuals in a case of emergency. I confess
I felt an exalted pleasure in this idea; and
could have wished it had been in my power to
have been of greater service on the occasion.
I however passed a sleepless night, being very
restless the whole time, and wishing for the
dawn of day long before its appearance; but
alas! the morning, which I had thought so
slow in its approaches, brought for me new
sources of grief and trouble; for on its arrival
I was found extremely ill, and for nearly three
years I was confined to my bed from this
period, with violent pains in all my limbs: my
symptoms were very severe, being for many
months completely deprived of the natural use
of my limbs, suffering great agony at times;
and but seldom free from acute pain for any

length of time together. The medical gentlemen who attended me, were completely baffled in their attempts to remove the cause of my complaint; all their kind efforts to restore my health were unsuccessful; although every means that medical skill could suggest, as likely to be beneficial to me, were tried and persevered in, yet all seemed of no avail.

In sickness the imagination is disturbed, and disagreeable, sometimes terrible ideas are apt to present themselves; and whether real or imaginary, occasion, for the time being, every variety of distress and pain. Such I fully experienced, in the restless nights of my long and painful illness: for, when the body is uneasy, the mind will be disturbed by it; and disagreeable ideas of various kinds, will, in sleep, be the natural consequences.

At this melancholy period, I was much alarmed, by dreaming three successive nights that my dear mother was dead, which I communicated to the Rev. P. Hersent at the time; but no great attention was paid to what forcibly struck me as an admonitory warning; it being considered merely the effect of perturbed imagination, and groundless fear; and consequently was disregarded. It, however, wonderfully affected my mind, nor could I in my then weak state, any way get rid of the impression it had made; it preyed on my mind; and added to my bodily afflictions.

It was not long, however, before these forebodings, (imaginary or real, call them what you please,) to my sorrow, were too soon realized: Madame, my mother, going to provide something for my use, fainted away on the stairs; where she remained sometime without assistance. Being alarmed at the long absence of my parent, so unusual, my dreams at once rushed into my mind, with increased horror; but what to do in this miserable situation, I knew not; unable to leave my bed, or walk a step when out of it, I immediately began making as much noise as possible, with the chairs nearest me, in hopes to attract the attention, and endeavour to induce any casual passenger, who might accidentally pass by the door, to come in to ascertain the cause; not doubting, if I obtained this point, we should soon be enabled to obtain necessary assistance. When I was nearly exhausted by my repeated efforts, I at length succeeded in attracting the notice of some person, who on entering the house, found my dear parent in an apparently lifeless state, extended on the stairs; this humane person did every thing in his power to restore suspended animation; and immediately sent for Messrs. Ch.pm.n & Br.yn., who not being at home, Mr. C. Br.ckw.ll was requested to attend, and who promptly gave his assistance, and partially restored animation to my poor parent, who was in this melancholy state brought up into the same room where I lay: myself nearly dead with fear and apprehension, from the state of suspense and miserable anticipation of its fatal result; the shock was almost too violent for me to bear, and had such a powerful effect on my weak and exhausted frame, that I was almost driven to despair; and indeed should have been, had not religion in some degree calmed my poignant and wretched feelings. My prayers were made to the Omnipotent unceasingly, for the restoration, through his divine mercy, of my miserable parent, whose remaining days in this world were but few in number; the allotted span of her life was nearly completed, and in the short space of three days my dear mother was no more; having departed this life on the first day of June, 1813.

Thus was I left a wretched orphan in a foreign country, quite unacquainted with the English language, confined to my bed by a long and painful illness, my mother dead by my side, myself unable to provide the most trifling thing towards the support of my existence: yet constantly relying on the bounty of an allwise and merciful creator, innumerable friends were raised up to protect, succour, and assist me, in my great distress and affliction. Even previously to the decease of my mother, the Rev. Mr. L.nc.st.r, with his accustomed benevolence, and the Rev. E. G. W.lf.rd, (the latter gentleman was at the time Mayor of Banbury,) called on the principal ladies of this Borough, and most humanely made the Baroness' then afflicted state known to them.— This benevolent appeal was not made in vain; donations of ten shillings and sixpence each, and in some instances one pound, were immediately made for our relief. Mrs. D'Oyley kindly contributed twenty pounds: the total amount of these benevolent gratuities was placed in the hands of P. O. B.gn.ll, Esq. and the most liberal and prompt relief afforded us in this pressing emergency; and after the decease of my affectionate parent, I received ten shillings per week for a long time from this charitable source, at the hands of this same gentleman, even without then knowing to whom I was indebted for this gratuitous and invaluable supply in my miserable situation; but to whom now I beg to return my most sincere and grateful thanks for the liberal munificence thus afforded me, in the time of my greatest need.

The reverend gentlemen before mentioned, recommended me to the particular notice and care of Mrs. M. L.ng., who kindly attended to their benevolent solicitations, and frequently visited me in my distress, assisting in a pecuniary way, and pouring consolation into my afflicted heart as copiously as the imperfect knowledge she had of the French language, would permit. To this lady I am indebted for innumerable benefits since received.—Such conduct to a stranger, surely bespeaks the true christian! Such actions require no elucidation; no comment of mine would equal their desert: or could it equal my gratitude for such signal benefits conferred, and so long continued.

This humane lady attended with the Rev. P. Hersent, to the preparations for the funeral; and followed as chief mourner the corpse of my deceased parent to church. and saw it deposited in the silent grave. The whole was conducted with the utmost decorum, suitable to the wishes of my deceased mother, a plain neat funeral without pomp; whose most earnest desire for a long time previously had been to share the grave of her departed husband; after which, Mrs. M. L.ng. returned to comfort and support me by every means in her power, to calm my distressed mind, to reconcile me, as far as it was practicable, to my irrecoverable loss, and soothe my afflictions, which she was so eminently gifted to perform, if within the reach of mortal comfort to accomplish.

The Rev. Mr. L . nc , . ter came to offer me aid and assistance at this most afflicting period, and afforded me consolation which greatly relieved me in my distressing situation. To this gentleman also my most grateful acknowledgements are ever due, for his kind intercessions in my behalf.

Lady, R . ggs M . ll . r was extremely kind to me at this period, and has uniformly continued her benevolence to the present time ; to her ladyship also, under divine Providence, I consider myself idebted for my restoration to health, in consequence of her continually sending me medicines, and affording me pecuniary assistance at the same time. Nothing could exceed the benevolence and humanity with which these numerous benefits were conferred, or the delicate manner in which they were presented ; very far exceeding any encomiums I am capable of adducing ; in fact, they exceed all praise.—Such distinguished munificence will ever claim my warmest acknowledgments of gratitude, and will never be effaced from my memory during my existence.

Mrs. Cr . wf . rd, Mrs. H . yw . rd, Mrs. W. st, Mrs. R . sh . r, and Miss E . t . n were particularly assiduous and attentive friends to me ; and therefore I beg to return my most sincere thanks to them.

The expence of my mother's funeral was defrayed by the generous benevolence of sundry humane individuals ; to whom I am under infinite obligations. — Such worthy acts of humanity will, I confidently trust, hereafter meet with their just reward; when all the pomp and splendour of this world will be deemed, in reality as vanity and dross.

I was under the necessity of selling the remaining few articles of furniture, books, &c. in my possession, to satisfy as far as they would go, the claims of my creditors; but they produced but a very small sum. After the sale I was removed to Mr. Garret's apartments, which had been previously taken for me, and where I still remain. His most Christian Majesty the king of France sent me eight pound sterling, from his residence at Hartwell-House. The late Queen (Charlotte) of England likewise sent me a donation of five pounds.

Richard Lorentz, Esq. from Hesse Cassel, in Germany, by my request received my pension, (allowed by the French Government,) and regularly remitted quarterly the amount, which was a great relief to me in my distress.

The Rev. E. G. W.lf.rd always kindly interested himself in my welfare; writing letters for me to many persons in office, &c. and through his interest the late Right Hon. the Earl of G..lf..d munificently relieved me in my difficulties, through the hands of W. W.lf.rd, Esq.

As soon as I was recovered from my long and painful illness, I employed myself in making fancy articles, &c. which were sold, to enable me to acquire something towards my support, by my own industry: but being still very weak, I could not do much in this way for sometime, yet every trifle gained was of service to me; and afterwards I added other branches in succession.

Mrs. B. Apl . in was a very kind friend, affording me every assistance in my distresses, assuaging my grief, and kindly relieving my perturbed mind in my illness. The Misses C . bb were also very affectionate to me, constantly interesting themselves in my welfare, and promoting my interest on all occasions; in fact, (like most of my friends) they endeavoured to amuse me in every way they could suggest, which I believe had no small share in calming my spirits; and which in the end was productive of much improvement in my health.

My kind benefactress Mrs. M. L . ng ., was indefatigable in affording me every necessary comfort, and extremely liberal in her very kind assistance to me at this period; as I was so very weak and nervous from my long confinement, the society of such a friend was of infinite service to me in every respect : and it is with the deepest sense of gratitude I treasure up in my mind, and often reflect on the innumerable kindnesses I have received in a foreign country; left as I was in the most unprotected state; but fortunately, in a country renowned in the annals of the world for magnanimity and generosity; of which I indeed have had practical and evident proofs; and for the truth of which, I can confidently and impartially speak, having in innumerable instances experienced the same, as will evidently appear on the perusal of this unvarnished narrative of facts; which requires no metaphorical diction, no ornamental or figurative style, to cou-vince any impartial person of the truth of my positions.

At this period I now turned my attention to the platting of willow, straw, and paper, for the manufacturing of bonnets, &c. likewise the knitting of gloves, for different friends; also plain sewing, and needle-work, which fully occupied my time: but all this was unproductive of much gain.

F. Wy_kh_m, Esq. and P. O. B_gn_ll, Esq. made repeated applications to different parties, for the recovery of a small sum of money due to me in Germany; but unfortunately without succeeding in their benevolent intentions: not any part of it could at this period be obtained, although every legal means were used, that could be deemed likely to effect this desirable object, or furnish a ground for future claims.

Going to the chapel at Overthorpe one morning, I fortunately formed an acquaintance with a catholic family, (Mrs. Pl_tf_rd's,) and received an invitation to her house at Adderbury, to meet Mrs. M_nn_ng, of Deddington, her sister; to whom she very kindly introduced me, and from whom I have since received many signal benefits. Mrs. Pl_tf_rd's father had been in France for nearly twelve years; they very kindly interested themselves in my behalf, obtained the assistance of several of their own friends, and also accommodated me with the loan of small sums at different times. I am likewise much indebted to them for their recommendation to a most invaluable friend, Mrs. H_pc_ft, with whom I have been particularly intimate for several years; which in

its consequences, has been of inestimable service to me : in fact, the whole family have
been constant and valuable friends to me up
to the present period : I am therefore under
the greatest obligations to them for their
invariable and continued kindness. Mrs.
H . pc . . ft has most indefatigably exerted herself in procuring, through her interest and
voluntary exertions, a considerable proportion
of the subscribers to my work, amounting to
upwards of one hundred names. This lady
still continues kindly to persevere for me, with
an expectation of still increasing this number.—
The pains and trouble thus taken to promote
my interest, have been wonderful, great beyond
expectation ; and for which my warmest acknowledgements of gratitude and thanks are
but a poor return : it is however my consolation to believe, that such benevolent and
charitable acts will meet with ample reward
hereafter ; such infinite reward, as will crown
her virtuous and truly christian charity.

To Mrs. T . yl . r I am likewise under great
obligations ; also to the Rev. Mr. C . rb . shl . y,
whose spiritual and temporal advice on many
occasions, has been of the greatest benefit to me ; proceeding from the pure motive
of doing good, influencing my actions much to
my future benefit and temporal welfare : indeed
this gentleman has been a truly valuable friend
to me in all circumstances. As has also the
Rev. Mr. Ch . rd . n, of Br . yles, and the Rev.
Mr. P . ns . ll, of M . . ch . . t . r ; to whom likewise I am infinitely indebted.

The Mayor of Banbury having received
information one morning that the Duchess of

L

of Oldenburg would, in the course of the day, pass through this borough, accordingly waited on her Grace, to pay those marks of personal respect and honour, due to the exalted rank and family of this illustrious personage. The ladies of Banbury with myself, waited on the Duchess ; the interview was short, as her Grace could not be prevailed on to leave the carriage ; but very kindly presented me with two pieces of gold, contained in a small box, at the same time recommending me to see the Duke of Oldenburg, who was expected to pass through this place on his route to Oxford : but we were extremely disappointed in this particular, a different route having been taken ; which deprived me of the anticipated pleasure of seeing this august personage, whom I was more particularly anxious to see, as my uncle Charles died in the service of the Duke, in the last war.

It has been generally acknowledged that the French Revolution has materially changed the face of society, and given a new and different impulse to the course of human affairs ; particularly in a land moistened with the blood of an amiable prince, and his faithful adherents : which caused those memorable vicissitudes, that have been exhibited to astonished Europe.—The titles of the nobility were abolished, and imprisonment and death were the order of the day, in my devoted country. The vigilant eye of the police at Paris, was constantly on the watch, to scrutinize into the actions of every foreigner, and penetrate, if possible, his most secret thoughts.—The diabolical system of spies was carried to such a length, that every action inimical to government, was registered, and resorted to as occasion required, or caprice dictated: the multitude of people employed by the police, was incredible.—A visit to a countryman in prison, was deemed a high misdemeanor, and was registered accordingly.

It is necessary to remark, that in no other country are the women so persevering, when they undertake to ask a favour of government, as in France; few being disconcerted at the first or second refusal, and many having been known to continue their efforts with such persevering zeal in the cause they undertake, that not unfrequently have they ultimately succeeded.—In this case, therefore, they wished if possible to lead back to their society a valiant people, whom the concussions of the revolution had thrown, as it were, at a distance from them; and by this means to restore that character of urbanity, which had been nearly, if not totally lost, in the struggles of party.

It must be confessed, that if the French people formerly possessed the graces of Athens, they had latterly exchanged them for a considerable degree of Spartan bluntness. And the examples of such men, whose minds had been but perhaps slightly cultivated, with the influence on the rising generation, whose education had been much interrupted, or materially altered, during the horrors of war, nay, from day to day, brought about a still greater change in the national character.—What has most effectually opposed this increasing evil? doubtless the society of amiable women; they impress the sentiments of decorum; they are the true preceptors, in elegance and refinement

L 2

taste: they restored the graces which had for-
saken us, brought back that affability which
was our distinguishing characteristic, and re-
created (if I may be allowed so to express myself) that nation, whom so many convulsions,
crimes, and misfortunes, had thrown out of its
true bias. Ah! had the chiefs of terror more
truly appreciated them, much less blood would
have flowed. Men who know how to prize
them as they ought to be prized, are rarely
barbarians. I cannot refrain mentioning an
instance of devoted female intrepidity, in what
she considered the cause of her country. In
the beginning of July, a female of the name of
Charlotte de Cordé, proceeded from Caen, in
Normandy, in the department of Calvados:
this person concerted the daring project of
delivering her country from those, whom she
considered as its enemies and its tyrants.
Among the jacobin party, none had rendered
themselves more obnoxious than Marat. On
the 12th, she wrote to solicit an interview with
that deputy, pretending that she had something
of high importance to communicate. As she
did not receive an immediate answer, she
addressed a second *billet*. And on the evening of
the 13th, she waited upon him again. Being
admitted, she entered into conversation with
him concering the supposed conspiracy which
existed at Caen, and the conspirators who had
fled thither. Marat answered, that the traitors
would soon be discovered, and at a day not
very distant, would lose their heads on a scaffold. He had scarcely uttered these words,
little thinking he should so soon expiate his
crimes and be numbered with the dead, when
observing a favourable opportunity, this female

plunged a dagger in his breast, and walked calmly out of the room. Upon her being secured, to which she made no resistance, this intrepid heroine was asked who were her accomplices? She answered, "I have none; no person has prompted me to perform the noble action which I have done: and if people will but take pains to examine into all the events preceding and subsequent to the death of Marat, they will be convinced that my sole motive was to free my country from its most dangerous enemy; to prevent, if possible, the rest of France being consumed by the fire of civil war; which was the avowed intention of this man.—I have voluntarily sacrificed my life, for the good of my country.—May peace be restored as speedily as I desire! I confess that I was obliged to have recourse to artifice, in order to gain admittance to this monster, but I could not otherwise have succeeded; and, therefore, I shall be happy to meet the fate I well know is destined for me."—And which she did with the greatest composure.

The principal agents in the events of this period had been accused of stupid pride and fatal policy; —of incapacity either to make or preserve peace; —of prodigality, in the idle waste of the blood and treasure of the state;— of overturning wantonly the governments of other countries;— of listening only to the voice of contemptible and perfidious flatterers;—of harbouring the most malignant passions;—of corruption, and of being ignorant of any force but that of bayonets. Their agents were mostly subaltern tyrants; spreading terror and consternation throughout the kingdom. Commerce, and the

useful arts were in a state of decay,—public
credit annihilated,—property insecure,—personal safety at the controul of these petty
tyrants,—civil and religious institutions in-
sulted and persecuted,—and liberty of speech
proscribed, under a very thin veil of hypoth-
esis:—treading underfoot the laws, and the
most inviolable principles of public and private
security,—of suffering no opposition to their
will,—of tormenting the people in every possible
mode,—of being, in short, despots and petty
tyrants in every sense of the words.

I might relate sufferings that would almost
exceed belief, and at the bare mention of which,
humanity would shudder;—wantonly inflicted by
order of these miscreants. I shall ever recollect
with humble gratitude, the first gleam of hope
and comfort, that shot across the gloom of my
poor father's confinement, when a state prisoner
in the dungeon of St. Pelagic. Religion
inspired him with the heart-cheering idea, that
neither massive walls, nor tremendous bolts,
and horrid chains, nor all the vigilance of
suspicious keepers, could conceal him from the
sight of God; all their cruelties and wanton
injustice, heaped upon him with such subtle
and persevering acrimony, sunk into oblivion
at the thought, and which he fondly cherished;
this afforded him infinite consolation in his long
imprisonment, and principally contributed to
enable him to support with a degree of
fortitude and resignation, (at which he has
since frequently expressed his wonder, and that
for so long a period as five years and a half,)
his at one time almost solitary confinement.
Ever obliged to be on his guard in all he said
or did; uncertain of his own destiny, and for a

long time that of his family ; ignorant of what passed beyond the walls of his prison, constantly ruminating on the severity of his unhappy fate, to which he saw no end : but inspired by his religious hopes, he endeavoured to resist the horrors of his long imprisonment, with an invincible and manly fortitude ; his spirit, truly heroic and undeviating, trusting solely to the will and mercy of that Omnipotent Being, whose inscrutable dictates are wisely ordained beyond the reach of mortal scan. He has been frequently heard to express his regret, at the cruel destiny of many of the old officers, as well as at that of himself, remaining in obscurity, who had honourable testimony to produce of what they have done and suffered for their native land, in innumerable instances : but now, thank heaven, their condition is much ameliorated, by the return of our beloved monarch to the throne of his ancestors ; and they confidently hope time will reinstate them in their ancient rights and priviliges. Under these considerations, may our souls be penetrated with the most lively gratitude, the most ardent love, and the most constant praise, to our glorious benefactor : we shall have daily reason to acknowledge his paternal care, although in this world all pleasures are mixed with pain, and perfect happiness cannot be found : yet have we great reason to be thankful for this most propitioous event.

The dreadful effects of the revolutionary system is too recent, to be in the least degree forgotten ; scarcely a family that has not lost some of its members by the troubles which it produced ; and many a family has not a member left, to reprobate the monsters who exercised this destructive fury; the scenes of blood which have flown, will not allow me to speak with coolness, on such an occasion.

Monsieur de V... was cast into prison in common with most of the other respectable people in France, at a moment when every person who had the misfortune to be of noble birth, or possessed of much property, was marked out for the victims of the revolution: while in confinement, he reflected that if he shared the fate of many of his fellow-prisoners who were led to execution, his whole fortune would be confiscated, and his children become beggars; but, that, if he should terminate his life while in confinement, as his children were minors, their inheritance could not legally be seized or confiscated, and that perhaps he should shorten the period of his existence a few hours only. These considerations were so powerful in his mind, that humbly praying for pardon from the Omnipotent, he effected his purpose; and thus secured his property to his children, by the sacrifice of his own life. Yet the crime of suicide admits of no extenuation; no person having a right to take away that life, but the divine Creator, who bountifully bestowed it.

A decree was passed, for transporting from the kingdom, such of the priests, or non-juring clergy, &c. who had not taken the civic oath, and for their property to be confiscated. The distress and misery which many worthy individuals suffered, in consequence of this despotic act, cannot be sufficiently deplored.—Many of these victims of conscience were hurried from

their friends and connections, and landed destitute and pennyless on a foreign shore: some
were committed to prison, others massacred;
and no inconsiderable number were reserved
for butchery in the capital.

It will remain to the latest ages a monument
of British hospitality and liberality, that some
thousands of these unhappy fugitives, ecclesi-
asticks and others, were received into England.
No prejudices could stifle the voice of humanity, or eradicate from the hearts of Britons,
that generosity which has always been the
characteristic of the nation:—they were not
only generously received, but treated with the
greatest humanity, and furnished with a safe
asylum from their implacable enemies; their
wants were supplied, and their miseries alleviated, and a stipendiary allowance granted them,
by the munificence of government, for their
support, during the time of their residence in this
country. Some of these persons, from choice, still
continue residents here, and will most probably
end their days in a kindom, which, under divine
Providence, had perhaps been the means of
preventing their destruction in their native land,
by their then infatuated countrymen.

How admirable is the providence of God,
and his tender care for our preservation! He
has numbered the days and years of us all.
How tranquil then ought we to be, and how
fearless of death! If we are interested in the
mediation of Jesus Christ, we may rest assured
that we shall not be taken out of the world till
we are ripe for eternal glory. Let us be animated to finish our appointed work in the years
we are likely to live, since we know not what

a day may bring forth. How wise, therefore,
will it be, to make an early preparation for that
death, which may surprise us in a moment!
Let us live, then, prepared to meet death ; that
come when it will, it may find us watchful ;
and that we may, even in our last moments,
triumph over it, through the mediation of our
blessed Saviour.

I cannot refrain paying my just tribute of
praise to the memory of the unfortunate re-
fugees from my own country, in this hospitable
kingdom, most of whom were persons of rank ;
they are deserving of general respect, but from
me a tribute of gratitude is due to them. I
felt for their misfortunes with no common sen-
sibility ; because though they have laboured
under the persecutions of oppressive power and
obloquy, I have yet experienced great kindness
from many of them. This testimony I owe to
truth.

I consider myself much indebted to Mrs.
Cr.wf.rd, who was my constant companion in
my afflictions ; and through whose acquaintance
I became known to Mrs. F..ld, of Adderbury,
who was so kind as to call on me at different
times, and afterwards made me an offer of a
residence at Adderbury, in a cottage of theirs,
in which a poor family was placed, to live with,
assist, and wait on me. I was subsequently
received as companion to Mrs. F..ld, which
was a fortunate circumstance for me at this
period, being destitute of money, and scarcely
knowing how to act. Lady M.H.r being
informed of this circumstance, with her usual
goodness sent, unknown to me, a new set of
clothes for my use ; which were of the greatest

service to me at this time; but the many obligations I am under to this benevolent lady, I am wholly unable adequately to describe; her kindness has in innumerable instances been continued up to the present period. For nearly three years I also experienced great kindness in the family of Mrs. F..ld, and felt it a duty incumbent on me, to assist and make myself serviceable to this benevolent lady, to the utmost in my power; who kindly introduced me to the acquaintance of many of the respectable inhabitants of Adderbury, and its vicinity: to Mr. and Mrs. M.lls, Mrs. Cl.rs.n, Miss Cl.rk., Miss S.m..sk.ll, Mrs. F.rd, Mrs. R.b.ns.n and family, who have all been very great friends to me in my adversity: likewise to W! F..ld, Esq. and family, whose invariable kindness merits my warmest acknowledgments of gratitude. Also to Capt. Adk.ns, Mrs. W..lst.n, the Rev. Mr. N.tt, Mr. Pl.tf.rd and family, Mrs. G.dd.rd, Miss G.dd.rd, Mr. W.ls.n, Mr. H.yn.s, Mr. John W.ll..ns, and many other valuable acquaintances in the neighbourhood. I am under great obligations to Mrs. F..ld, for thus adding to the circle of my friends and acquaintance, as also for innumerable benefits I received, during my residence at Adderbury, which will never be effaced from my memory.

It was with great reluctance I left Mrs. F..ld's, but being rather in embarrassed circumstances, it induced me to live in a more retired way; the expences necessary to appear in such genteel company, being beyond what my limited means would allow. I therefore came to Banbury, and enquired for my old lodgings at Mr. Garret's, which were immediately granted to me as formerly; to whom I am much obliged, and in fact, to the whole family, who have at all times acted with the greatest kindness to me, under all circumstances.

When Mrs. F..ld became acquainted with the circumstances of my leaving her, regretting the loss of my company, she kindly offered to take me as an inmate in her house; but my determination was fixed, I therefore declined accepting this kind proposal; although I received every mark of kindness from them, since my return to Banbury.

During my stay at Adderbury, I had unavoidably contracted some debts, which I had no means of paying, in consequence of my small pension being wholly inadequate to meet these demands; and although at certain times I received presents, &c. from my friends, yet I was never able to discharge these accumulating demands; and have been obliged in one instance to pay 5 per cent. per annum interest, on the amount of my bill for grocery, &c. until I should discharge the principal, to prevent legal proceedings, with which I had been frequently threatened by this same individual. Many other of my creditors, as a matter of course, applied to me for the payment of their debts, on my leaving Adderbury, but were induced to wait until I should be enabled to pay them, and which is the main object of this publication; the profits of which will be applied to the payment of all my creditors; and which I trust by divine Providence, and through the kind interest of my invaluable friends, I' shall be enabled wholly to effect. This paramount duty could only induce me to undertake a work of this kind, being too well aware of my total inability to attempt any thing of importance in the literary way, owing in a great measure to the unpardonable neglect of my education ; but, as I said before, I have every thing to hope from the kind indulgence and candour of my friends, and the generous liberality of the public ; who, though they will find but little Attic salt in these Memoirs, will yet, I trust, appreciate the motives which urged me onwards in this attempt.

My most anxious wish for leaving Adderbury, was by my own exertions and industry, to endeavour, if possible, to provide for myself ; and devise some means, if practicable, to pay off my incumbrances. I called on all my friends to gain every information I could from them, how to act in this dilemma. I was advised by Mrs. T.yl.r and other friends, to publish, by subscription, the memoirs of my parents, and my own eventful life ; as the most likely mode of succeeding : who at the same time offered me every assistance, but as I was undetermined, not knowing precisely how to act, from the variety of plans proposed by my friends, it was for that time deferred, for future consideration.

At this period, a French lady who had been accustomed to visit the Rev. Mr. H.rs.nt, at Overthorpe, annually, and who had (like myself) experienced a large share of trouble and afflictions, came to reside at Overthorpe. I met this unfortunate person at the chapel, who informed me she had much uneasiness on her

mind, having been greatly deceived by her
reputed friends, whom she had left in the
occupation of a house in London, on the
liberal condition of their paying only the poors'
rates, taxes, &c. which they wholly neglected
to do; and that in consequence of this neglect,
the furniture, &c. was seized, to satisfy these
demands. It was therefore necessary that she
should be present, to mitigate, or if possible, to
prevent the more expensive consequences. She
anxiously wished me to go with her, which at
length I agreed to do; but was obliged to
borrow a small sum of money, to defray the
expences of the journey; which we undertook
by the cheapest mode of conveyance, namely,
the waggon: it was, however, a very tedious
way of travelling, being two days and three
nights on the road, in the inclement season of
winter, about Christmas. On our arrival in
town, we were under the unpleasant necessity
of sleeping in a bed which had not been used
for many months, belonging to a French gentleman, who had returned to France, and who
rented this room; which had been occupied by
no one during his absence, but was usually
paid for by him regularly at stated periods,
although not occupied. We were farther
obliged to live in a miserable back-kitchen,
every pane of glass in the window of which
being broken, or wholly out; a blanket being
the substitute for a curtain, to the shattered
window. In this wretched place we remained
seven weeks, until the unfortunate business
was accommodated and settled in the best
manner we could accomplish.

I endeavoured during my stay in town, to

find out the residence of some old friends of my parents, and fortunately succeeded in meeting with Madame la Comtesse de Callone, who kindly introduced me to the notice of Monsieur Nettement, and the Marquis de B.rt..tt; through whose interest I obtained the payment of a small sum of money, left to me by a great uncle, in France; and who also kindly procured for me, the certificate of marriage of my parents, at Le Quesnoy, and my certificate of baptism; for which I had repeatedly applied previously without success. Monsieur Nettement called on me at this deplorable residence, to obtain every necessary information respecting my pecuniary difficulties, offering to use his interest in procuring for me, if to be obtained, the remaining sums due to me in France and Germany: and to whose persevering benevolence I am much indebted. I experienced the greatest kindness also from the Comtesse de Callone, who has been truly indefatigable in whatever would tend to promote my welfare; and without whose kind solicitude and attention, I should doubtless have experienced many greater privations:—this lady has afforded me the best advice and assistance in the trying times of adversity and trouble; and her great kindness has been invariably continued to the latest period; and for which, I wish to express those sentiments of gratitude, which I have and ever shall retain, for her goodness to me, during this benevolent lady's stay in England; who wrote to me but a few days previously to her going to the continent, in the most friendly manner; and I have had occasion since, frequently to regret the irreparable loss I have sustained by her absence. Through the interest of my most benevolent benefactress, Monsieur le General Damien has taken the trouble personally to call on my aunt, at Cassel, in Germany, and has fully explained to her my present situation and circumstances, in order to forward my interest as much as possible in that quarter; and for which, my warmest acknowledgments are justly due.

Having a great desire to see the interior of the Convent of the Benedictines, I begged the favour of Madame Courtois to go with me to Hammersmith, for that purpose. The Mother Abbess kindly explained to me the nature of the institution, and shewed me the different apartments, &c. Having a wish, at some future time to embrace a religious life, I took the liberty to ask if they would be inclined to take me as a *religeuse*, if I wished to enter, for the annual receipt of my pension; and which would, I doubt not, have been acceeded to:—I further wished to know what sum would be charged for six weeks, if I should wish to make trial of the order for that time; this was offered to be done gratuitously: but being embarrassed with debts, I could not conscientiously accept this liberal offer, until I was enabled to pay my numerous creditors. I was much pleased with my visit, and have an inclination, at a future period to carry my intended design into effect, and retire into the privacy of a convent; when I shall fully have accomplished the total discharge of my present incumbrances, and pecuniary embarrassments. On this subject, which will occupy my most serious thoughts and attention, I purpose taking the advice of my friends, and to decide accordingly.

While in London, I received a very kind letter from Mrs. F..ld, expressing her anxiety for my future welfare, and soliciting my early return, as soon as the business I had undertaken was finished. This lady likewise requested Miss Cl.rk., who was going to town, to endeavour to find me, and personally to communicate to me her wishes for my immediate return; which I did accordingly, as soon as I could with propriety leave Madame Courtois. Mrs. W.st twice favoured me with a call at this deplorable place, and kindly invited me to her house, but I could not avail myself of her kind offer, being at such a considerable distance from Duke Street, Lincoln's Inn Fields, otherwise I should have been pleased to accept it.

Not having the means to pay the coach fare, I was obliged to content myself in returning by the waggon; and most tedious did I find this journey. On my return, however, I felt still more miserable, as several of my creditors on my arrival, called on me, and insisted on being paid their respective demands; but alas! I had no money to enable me to comply: some of them were so very angry at my inability to pay them, as to threaten me repeatedly with imprisonment, and to seize the few goods remaining in my possession. I was, therefore, under the necessity of availing myself of the kind offer of my most invaluable friend, M... F...ld, to come to her house; and which I did, by being provided with a key of the garden door, by the back way, for the sake of privacy; and more particularly on Thursday, being market days, when I have often times been

M

obliged to leave the town, and go into the country at some distance, to my friends, to avoid the incessant duns of my clamorous creditors. On these urgent occasions, I generally went to Mrs. H.pcr.ft's, Mrs. T.yl.r's, or Mrs. M.nn.ng's, all of whom well knew my troubles and afflictions; and invariably afforded me every comfort in their power, kindly assuaging my distress, and administering to my necessities on all occasions; which certainly very greatly relieved my agonized mind.

The Rev. Mr. W.M.lls, having occasion to go to Germany, very kindly offered to exert himself in my behalf, by promoting my interest to the utmost in his power, and endeavouring to procure for me, a remittance of some part at least, of the property due to me; but after repeated unsuccessful applications, nothing could at this time be obtained: but on quitting the country, he kindly left the management of my affairs in the hands of a very respectable friend of his, who took a great deal of pains in this respect, on my account; but without being productive of the desired effect. At the same time we gained one material point by their joint assistance and perseverance, namely, the establishment of my claim; which was recognized by the other parties concerned, and which affords rational ground to hope for our ultimately succeeding in recovering it.

This was a great consolation to me; but from the repeated delays, and the impatience of some of my creditors to have their demands liquidated, to bring the matter as early as possible to legal issue, I was induced to employ a soliditor, and Mr. T . ms kindly offered to undertake the business; who, after repeated applications, and paying due attention in conforming to the precise forms required in the documents, had good ground to hope that he should procure for me about forty pounds; which but for the gratuitous exertions of this gentleman, most probably I should never have been able to have obtained.

Since my long and painful illness, I have never enjoyed so good a state of health as formerly; of that invaluable blessing, of which I had previously possessed no small share, I am now doomed to lament the want, frequently experiencing continued indisposition : on these occasions, I have generally applied to Mr. Br.yn., who has always afforded me the most prompt medical aid; and has not unfrequently succeeded in preventing a relapse of my former complaints, which indicating symptoms had led us to expect would otherwise have been the unavoidable result.—This gentleman has afforded me gratuitous attendance with the utmost regularity, equal to what could have been given, had I been in different circumstances, and been enabled to remunerate such meritorious services; which, however, this benevolent gentleman well knew was not the case, or at all probable that it ever would be.—For such disinterested generous conduct, continued for so many years without deviation, and for the many signal benefits I have received from this gentleman's skill, I cannot avoid expressing those sentiments of gratitude which I shall ever retain.

M 2

I have received great kindness from the late Mrs. T. W. lf. rd, and many of her friends, who afforded me every assistance in promoting the success of my present undertaking ; the loss of this benevolent lady, whose memory I shall ever revere, I do indeed most feelingly regret. To Mr. Gillet I beg to return my best thanks, for his kindness to me on all occasions. To Mr. J. Th. rn. I am much indebted, for the interest he has taken in my bahalf during his residence in London.

Mrs. F. .ld kindly invited me one day to join a party to the Marquis of Buckingham's seat, in order to view the curiosities and beauties of Stowe ; with which place I was much delighted, having never before seen any thing equal to it. We spent the whole day in minutely examining every part of this extensive and enchanting spot. While viewing the beautiful paintings, my attention was forcibly arrested by a very fine one of the late Marquis, who had been such a benefactor to my deceased parents and myself, and which so agitated my feelings, that the sensations of regret at the instant rushed on my mind so powerfully, that I was obliged to retire to another room, to compose my perturbed mind, and which I was unable to effect for some time ; but nothing can ever weaken the veneration and gratitude I shall ever retain for the memory of this august personage. I was extremely anxious not to disturb the harmony of the company by my indisposition, I therefore concealed it as far as possible, and by degrees assumed as much cheerfulness as I could command. The whole of our party was extremely pleased with the great variety and high value of the different works of art, which we met with here, and the delightful effect of the *tout en semble*. We returned highly gratified with our visit; and I have since had frequent occasion to relate to many of my friends, the particulars of this excursion, some of whom had seen, and others had never visited this splendid mansion.

I endeavoured, for some time, to form a collection of old china for Mrs. F..ld, and procured a tolerable quantity of various kind; but could not succeed to the extent of my wishes in this particular, from the scarcity of pieces to be met with of any value. I likewise attempted, at another period, to collect different species of curious birds, and various kinds of plants, herbs, &c. in which I was partially successful.

Being so highly delighted with my visit to Stowe, Mrs. F..ld invited me to go with a party of friends to Blenheim; and accordingly we proceed to the magnificent seat of the Duke of Marlborough, and were very politely admitted to see the interior of this splendid mansion. I was much pleased with the beautiful paintings, many of which appear highly valuable; I was quite charmed also with the fine collection of antique china, so elegantly and tastefully arranged in the china-house, containing many of the finest specimens I ever saw. The beautiful and scientific manner in which the grounds, &c. are laid out, attracted our particular attention; the wood and water afford views superbly grand and imposing; the immense edifice is likewise highly worthy of the attention of visitants; this splendid monu-

ment of the munificence of the English government to one individual, will remain to distant
ages a stimulus to the exertions of those men of
genius, who profess a military life, in this
kingdom. After a careful examination of the
whole, we returned, abundantly gratified with
our charming excursion.

A short time after, a second journey to the
same place was proposed; I had, therefore, an
opportunity of again visiting Blenheim, with a
party of friends, who opportunely arrived from
London, and who had never seen this delightful
residence. A pedestrian excursion, however,
was this time agreed upon; I accordingly left
Banbury early in the morning, to take breakfast
with my friends at Bodicott; from thence we
proceeded to Deddington, where we partook of
an early dinner; we then continued on our
journey to the Fox Inn, and after taking some
further refreshment, walked on to Sturdis
Castle, when unfortunately it began to rain,
which induced us to wish for some mode of
conveyance, to carry us the remainder of the
distance, but none could be procured; to add
to the dilemma, some of the party began to
feel much fatigued, being unaccustomed to
travel so great a distance on foot; however,
there was no alternative, and we were under
the necessity of walking on in the rain until
we reached Woodstock: here we remained
some time, and refreshed and dried ourselves,
at a cottage: at length we reached Blenheim,
where our fatigue vanished, in the pleasing
anticipation of viewing this magnificent abode.
We were, however, doomed to experience
further disappointment, having arrived too late

to be admitted to view the interior of the house; we were, therefore, obliged to console ourselves with examining the exterior.— We continued in the park until the approach of evening, when we retired to the Marlborough Arms Inn, and took up our abode for the night. We renewed our visit in the morning, and although disappointed in the first instance, we were now amply satisfied, and highly pleased with our excursion We returned the same day on foot to Deddington, and were kindly accommodated with beds for the whole party, at my friend Mrs. M.nn.ng's, being so much fatigued that we could not proceed any farther that day. I took the opportunity in the morning to visit a few friends; we then proceeded on our pedestrian excursion back to Bodicott; where I left my party, and returned to Banbury the same evening.

On our return home, a plan was arranged to visit Stowe in the same way. We therefore proceeded to Croughton-House, and were kindly provided with refreshment, by my most invaluable friend Mrs. H.pcr.ft, and obligingly invited to call again on our return. We now began to feel rather fatigued, and embraced the opportunity of going in a cart, which fortunately was passing at the time; the carrier being well known to us, we finished our journey in this manner to Buckingham. As we intended a kind of gypsey excursion, we had provided ourselves with provisions, &c. and alighted at the carrier's house, and regaled ourselves with what our stock afforded. We passed the night at the inn; in the morning we again paid a visit to the carrier, and partook of breakfast from our stores; after which, we proceeded in the same vehicle to Stowe, and agreed with the carrier to meet us at a time appointed, for our return. We then proceeded to view the house, &c. which afforded me increased satisfaction, although I had so recently seen it. The gardens, temples, &c. were again viewed with increased curiosity. The party was much amused in this excursion; but what particularly increased my admiration was, that a gentleman who accompanied us was able to give the most minute scientific description of every object we viewed; which was acknowledged by the person who generally attends the visitors here, and who said masked, that there had not, to his knowledge, been a person there for many years previously, who had so accurately and scientifically explained the whole. At the hour appointed, we returned in the carrier's cart to the Barley-mow, and reached Croughton-House the same evening, where we received the kindest treatment from my ever invaluable friend's there; whose hospitality and kind beneficence to me at all times, is beyond all praise. We reached Bodicott in the evening; after taking leave of the party, I walked on to Banbury: and the following morning we agreed to visit Wroxton-Abbey, which I had long wished to see, but had not a previous opportunity, although I received the greatest kindness from the late Earl and Countess of Gu.lf.rd: as did also my deceased parents. We accordingly made a party, and soon reached Wroxton; the venerable appearance of this ancient Abbey much pleased us; and it more particularly excited my admiration, from the munificence

experienced by our family from its late possessors ; to whose memory my warmest sentiments
of gratitude will be ever due. We continued
our promenades in the charming walks and
gardens, until the hour of dinner; we then
dined in the temple on the mount, highly
pleased with the delightful view from this
eminence. As in our former excursion, we
had taken our provisions with us, and provided
ourselves with wine ; but prefering wine and
water, we employed a little girl we took with
us, to procure some clear water for us in a
goblet; but soon after, we were much alarmed
by the cries of this young person, who had
filled her large glass with water from the
fountain, and in her return to us, had fallen
into the water ; I immediately, therefore, ran
to the spot, and succeeded in extricating her
from her perilous situation, but not without
getting wetted myself; but in consequence of
the charming state of the weather, being hay-
making time, we did not feel any ill effects
from this accidental ablution. The grotto,
Chinese-house, cascade, Tuscan temple, monument, and beautiful gardens, afforded us much
satisfaction ; and after highly enjoying our
pleasant ramble, we took tea at the porter's
lodge, and returned in the evening completely
satisfied with the amusements of the day.

A short time after this, Mrs. F. .ld invited
me to go with a party to the forest fair, which
was a complete novelty to me. We took
provisions with us, and partook of the amusements of the scene; but, unfortunately, the
rain coming on, we were obliged to retire to
the barouche, and partook of our frugal repast

therein; but when the servant unpacked the wine, we were much surprised to find the bottles broken, which obliged us to regale ourselves with water instead of wine; though this accident did not prevent our partaking of a comfortable refreshment; and we returned home late in the evening, much pleased with the variety of amusements of this *fête champêtre*.

On the celebration of peace between England and France, public rejoicings were held in most places: at Banbury the gentlemen and ladies of the place provided a public dinner, and tea party, in the horse-fair, in which the ladies kindly assisted the whole time; Mrs. M. L. ng., who had no small share in this voluntary duty, took me under her care, and placed me near her person at table, where I assisted to the utmost in my power in promoting the hilarity and festivity of the meeting. I also visited the celebration of the same auspicious event at Deddington, and partook of some of the roast beef, &c. and joined in the amusements of the day at that place.

I had the happiness to be informed, about this period, that I had two aunts still living in Germany; from one of whom, I received a very flattering and kind letter, promising to assist me in recovering my property there; and offering a small gratuity annually, which, however, I have not yet had the pleasure to receive; but am in expectation of its fulfilment. The latter aunt has made a claim to some part of the property due to me there, which I am fearful will reduce the remainder of my claim to a very small sum indeed.

Mr. T. ms in conformity to the arrangements previously made for the recovery of my claim in Germany, after taking a great deal of trouble in my behalf on this subject, at length succeeded in procuring for me forty pounds from this quarter; and after the deduction of the expences, (no charge whatever being made on his part,) I had the pleasure to receive thirty-seven pounds three shillings and four pence; without the benevolent exertions of this gentleman, I should in all human probability never have obtained this amount.—I wish, therefore, to express those sentiments of gratitude which I have and ever shall retain, for such generous conduct. On receipt of this sum, I was enabled to pay some of my creditors, particularly my most troublesome ones, and whose claims I immediately discharged out of this welcome supply.

Having waited upon Mrs. M. L. ng., for the purpose of asking her advice on the work I intended to undertake; this lady kindly offered me au asylum in her own house, until it should be completed; and which was proposed should be under her directions. She had the goodness further to extend her kindness to my friends, whom she welcomed at all times to her house, which was a source of great satisfaction to me; and I am sorry to say she had no inconsiderable share of trouble with some of my creditors: and has taken great pains to promote my interest in every way, by writing in my behalf to many persons of quality, and endeavouring to procure subscribers to my publication. Mrs. M. L. ng. has likewise kindly procured a friend to take

my portrait gratuitously, which will be presented with the work. — Such disinterested
generous conduct claims my warmest acknowledgements of gratitude; and I shall never
forget the very many and great obligations I
am under to this my most benevolent benefactress; for whose welfare my prayers are
daily made to that Omnipotent Being, whose
all-seeing eye penetrates the secrets of every
heart, and who will, I confidently trust, amply
reward such magnanimous conduct in futurity.

The Rev. Mr. P. Hersent, from the time
I came to England, has been my spiritual
dicector to the present hour; this gentleman
has taken a great deal of trouble on my account, in promoting my interest and welfare by
every means in his power; at all times affording me the best advice, and comforting my
afflicted mind, by his spiritual directions. His
character as a minister, a good man, and a true
christian, is indisputable, and highly praiseworthy: ever strict in the performance of every
religious duty, and eminently benevolent as far
as practicable. The limited means entrusted
to his disposal by divine Providence, are so
judiciously applied in charities, as to effect the
best purposes to which they could be directed.
To this benevolent, humane, and most worthy
minister, I am anxious to express those sentiments of gratitude, which I shall ever retain
for his invariable kindness to me on all occasions, whose mind and manners are so suitable
to his sacred function.

The total amount of my debts remaining at
the present period unpaid, is one hundred and

forty pounds twelve shillings and ten-pence;* which I have the unspeakable pleasure to anticipate, by the generous and liberal subscriptions received from my friends and the public, I shall be enabled wholly to discharge; this will be a source of infinite satisfaction to me, and has been the subject of my most anxious solicitude for a very long time past. The anticipation of fully accomplishing this most desirable object, has been the source of the greatest satisfaction to me, and its fulfilment will complete my happiness. I have before

---

* In consequence of the many delays which have protracted the publication of these Memoirs, the Baroness has unavoidably *increased* rather than lessoned the amount of her encumbrances; for in addition to *thirty three pounds and upwards*, which, resulting from her imperfect knowledge of the English language, she has been obliged to pay a person at Banbury, for assisting her in writing the manuscript, she has had other expenditures to meet, connected with her feeble undertaking. The individual to whose hands the correction of the manuscript and the revisal of the press have been intrusted, thinks it right also just to subjoin, that as a stranger to the Baroness de Poly, and from the imperfect state of the manuscript, he could not of his own accord make such alterations as he could otherwise have wished; still as the most material defects have been attended to, he trusts the reader will overlook verbal criticisms, and a few literary erratas.—The time and labour required, and which he has been obliged to bestow upon the work, in order to make it in any way fit for the public eye, have not been inconsiderable: in fact, it is almost impossible to calculate upon the many difficulties he has had to wade through, in order to complete his undertaking. Indeed, it was only the wish to benefit the subject of these Memoirs, that induced him to engage in a work, which, in a literary point of view, he feels assured, can afford him no commendation whatever.

The Editor is happy to add, that the above note is permitted by the Baroness, whom he has had the pleasure of seeing in Northampton, to accompany the work.

observed, that this was the principal motive to
my undertaking a work, I feel myself so inadequate to direct: I do, therefore, most
humbly solicit the kind indulgence of my
friends and the public; my sole intention
having been to relate a plain unvarnished
narrative of facts, without the aid of fiction.
My want of education in my youth has been
an insurmountable obstacle to my attaining
any literary knowledge, to which, therefore, I
can make no pretensions; but as my motive
is pure, my acknowledged want of a thorough
acquaintance with grammatical rules and the
idiom of the English language, I doubt not, will
plead my excuse with my friends, who are fully
acquainted with my disabilities; and yet whose
continued kindness to me on all occasions,
far exceeds all praise. I confidently repose
on the candour of a generous and discerning
public; having no doubt but that every indulgence which has been claimed, will be
readily allowed. And now having brought my
Memoirs to a close, when I take a retrospective
view on the past days of my life, even in the
earliest stage of infant weakness, I trace the
hand of divine Providence, whose arm has
helped, supported, protected, and defended me
through the dark scenes of adversity and
danger! The supreme Being has guided my
feet, and brought me from my own country,
into a strange land; where I have been surrounded with innumerable friends; who, like
the good Samaritan, have poured into my
wounded bosom the oil and wine of consolation and of love! Here let me pause, and
gratefully bless and adore my gracious benefactor, whose mercy and goodness has followed

me all the days of the years of my life long!
and who has put it into your hearts, my good
and generous, my honoured and revered subscribers and benefactors, to extend the helping-
hand to extricate me from my temporal difficulties, to shield me from distress, and place
me in an humble, yet independent state.   Accept the orphan's grateful acknowledgments.
My prayers shall ever be offered up at the
throne of grace, for your prosperity ; and may
the blessing of her you have saved from
perishing, rest upon you and your posterity for
ever!

FINIS.

ABEL, PRINTER, NORTHAMPTON

RETURN TO ➡

CIRCULATION DEPARTMENT
Main Library • 198 Main Stacks

LOAN PERIOD 1 HOME USE	2 **NRLF**	3
4	5	6

ALL BOOKS MAY BE RECALLED AFTER 7 DAYS.
Renewls and Recharges may be made 4 days prior to the due date.
Books may be Renewed by calling 642-3405.

DUE AS STAMPED BELOW

SENT ON ILL		
SEP 0 9 1997		
U. C. BERKELEY		

FORM NO. DD6

UNIVERSITY OF CALIFORNIA, BERKELEY
BERKELEY, CA 94720-6000

Im TheStory
personalised classic books

UNIQUE
GIFT

FOR KIDS, PARTNERS
AND FRIENDS

Timeless books such as:

Kids

Alice in Wonderland • The Jungle Book • The Wonderful Wizard of Oz
Peter and Wendy • Robin Hood • The Prince and The Pauper
The Railway Children • Treasure Island • A Christmas Carol

Adults

Romeo and Juliet • Dracula

Highly Customizable **Change** Books Title **Replace** Characters Names with your's **Upload** Photo for inside page! **Add** Inscriptions

Visit
Im TheStory .com
and order yours today!

Lightning Source UK Ltd.
Milton Keynes UK
UKHW052359101219
R2168700002B/R21687PG355034UKX11B/2/P